Our Heritage

D1739111

Our Heritage

The Past in the Present of African-American and African Existence

TSENAY SEREQUEBERHAN

ROWMAN & LITTLEFIELD PUBLISHERS, INC.
Lanham • Boulder • New York • Oxford

ROWMAN & LITTLEFIELD PUBLISHERS, INC.

Published in the United States of America
by Rowman & Littlefield Publishers, Inc.
4720 Boston Way, Lanham, Maryland 20706
http://www.rowmanlittlefield.com

12 Hid's Copse Road
Cumnor Hill, Oxford OX2 9JJ, England

British Library Cataloguing in Publication Information Available

Library of Congress Cataloging-in-Publication Data

Serequeberhan, Tsenay, 1952–
    Our heritage:the past in the present of African-American existence /
Tsenay Serequeberhan.
        p.   cm.
    Includes bibliographical references and index.
    ISBN 0-8476-8920-4 (cloth : alk. paper)—ISBN 0-8476-8921-2 (pbk : alk. paper)
    1. Afro-Americans—Historiography.   2. Afro-Americans—Ethnic identify.
    3. Afro-Americans—Race identity.   4. Civil rights movements—United States—
History—20th century.   5. Africans—Historiography.   6. Africans—Ethnic identify.
    7. Africans—Race identity.   8. Postcolonialism—Africa.   I. Title.
    E184.65.S47 2000
    973'.0496073'072—dc21   99-048901

♾ ™The paper used in this publication meets the minimum requirements of American
National Standard for Information Sciences—Permanence of Paper for Printed Library
Materials, ANSI/NISO Z39.48—1992

To the Eritrean People's Liberation Front and to all those who, sacrificing life and limb, have fought for and are still fighting for the complete emancipation of the African continent. It is in light of their endurance and sacrifice that our intellectual efforts have any sense or meaning.

This book is also dedicated to the kind memory of my father, Serequeberhan Gebrezgi, and to my two sons, Nesim-Netssere and Awate-Hayet, to the enduring heritage of the past and the hopeful possibilities of the future.

History will one day have its say; it will not be the history taught in the United Nations, Washington, Paris, or Brussels, however, but the history taught in the countries that have rid themselves of colonialism and its puppets. Africa will write its own history, and both north and south of the Sahara it will be a history full of glory and dignity.

Do not weep for me, my companion, I know that my country, now suffering so much, will be able to defend its independence and freedom. Long live the Congo! Long live Africa!

—Patrice Lumumba

The newly awakened people all over the world pose a problem for what is known as Western interests. . . . But the internal forces pose an even greater threat . . . when they have properly analyzed the situation and know what the stakes really are.

—Malcolm X

Contents

Preface: Existence and Heritage

Existence is always actualized in a specific and concrete heritage. Existence? The word derives from the Latin *exsistere: ex-*, out, plus *-sistere*, to cause to stand, set, place, to come forth, stand forth. Based on this we can say that that which exists is that which stands forth. A heritage, then, is the sedimented layering over time— that is, the life of a community—of the actuality of existence, which in "standing forth" does so necessarily in specific and determined ways and thus constitutes a heritage, a certain way of "being-in-the-world." And yet, to this day, most European thinkers write as if their heritage—the way their existence stands forth in being—is, for all that matters, coequal to existence as such!

This book is an attempt to bypass this constricted view and think of the actuality of black existence—African American and African—in terms of a limited number of seminal questions and figures that have marked the character of our heritage, that is, the actuality of our "standing forth."

The closing days of the twentieth century are a time focused on the diversity of human existence. Thus, the efforts of this study are centered on crucial aspects of the African American and African heritage: two organically interlinked moments of this diversity. The "effective past" and how it "shows" itself in the possibilities of African American and African exsistere—this is our basic concern.

Introduction: Africans and African Americans in the Present

$\mathbf{F}$rantz Fanon points out, quoting René Char, that "a poem is the assemblage in movement of determining original values, in contemporary relation with someone that these circumstances bring to the forefront."[1] Who is this "someone," and what are the "circumstances" in "contemporary relations" that bring her or him to the "forefront"? In David Diop's poem "Afrique," for example—in all that the poem says about enslavement, resistance, and the incremental and bitter actualization of liberty—or in Aimé Césaire's epochal poem *Return to My Native Land,*[2] who is it that is being addressed?

To be sure, as Plato noted long ago, "A poet, if he is to be a poet, must compose fables [and] not arguments."[3] And yet, as is well known, African poems, proverbs, sayings, fables, and so on are all condensed arguments that encapsulate, and hence conserve, the reasoned truth of a heritage, from one generation to the next.[4] Thus, in this book, Plato notwithstanding, we will be concerned not only with the condensed arguments preserved in the above-cited and similar poems but also with all that the struggle and poetry of the African liberation struggle and the dire struggle of African American life call us to or give us to understand.

Our concern, in other words, is focused on the ground or underlying historical edifice of lived experience—the actuality of a heritage—that structures and forms the bedrock out of which poems and their audiences arise. Our purpose is a philosophical exploration aimed not at poems as such but at the lived underpinnings that hermeneutically ground the force and appeal of such poems.

What is in these poems that compels our attention, even when we are critical of their "essentialism"? This, then, is the basic question that will orient our thinking in this study. To this end, the introduction will lay out the parameters of this exploration in the six chapters and conclusion that constitute this book.

I

For the first time today (the late 1990s) since the end of the nineteenth century, the African continent is completely independent. In itself this is a great achievement. This "independence," however, ill-fated at best, has not brought about the hoped-for freedom that was the object of the struggle in the late 1950s and early 1960s, the period of the first wave of political independence, or even in the 1970s and early 1990s, the second wave of African political independence.[5]

To explore this failure and its hoped-for but yet-to-be-actualized possibilities is the task of those of us concerned with Africa and its possible futures. This, however, is not equal to engaging in studied monographs, in effect monologues, on the "universal" and the "particular."[6] To explore our present, and its hoped-for possibilities, it is necessary in my view to at least commence by proposing an examination of our heritage as Africans in a postcolonial Euro-American-dominated world.

Analogously, on this side of the Atlantic, the gains of the civil rights movement—the analogue of the African struggle against colonialism—and the continuing struggles of people of color in general are under threat and constantly being challenged.[7] The minimal remedial achievements of black rights are being used as the scapegoat for all the ills of society. In short, racism—in all its forms—is still with us.[8]

What the struggle to end racism, the civil rights movement, did was to minimally curtail the blatant and official sanction of this odious phenomenon. In this context, we presently have the increase of police brutality in the inner cities,[9] the canceling of the remedial gains of civil rights legislation, and the systemic putting into question of black solidarity in highly publicized celebrity trials and government hearings for high office.[10] All of the above occurs while the flight of capital to sunnier climes, in search of cheap labor, is constantly undermining the livelihood of the racially and ethnically diverse working poor. Thus, the civil rights movement and its analogue, the African anticolonial struggle—both heroic, historic, and necessary movements—inspired much hope but managed to attain only minimal results. It is, then, within this context that the question of heritage has to be posed for African American and African existence, for this is the continental and global lived politico-economic milieu—that is, the inheritance—that frames our present.[11]

This kind of reflexive engagement is, in my view, a critical act of theoretic service. For our shared heritage, "whether we are expressly aware of it or not," is the "effective-history" that constitutes us as who we are in the present moment of time.[12] To this extent, to explore our heritage—the coagulated cluster of lived and efficacious prejudgments that constitutes our present—is to stake out and explore the possibilities of our "effective-history," the sedimented layering of our past that constitutes our present identity. For, as the Congolese philosopher Okonda w'oleko Okolo has correctly noted, our "cultural memory is ceaselessly renovated retroactively by new historic discoveries. Our past, by continually modifying itself through our scientific discoveries, summons us to newer appropriations [and] towards a better grasp of our identity."[13] It is to such a task that this text is devoted. For "our identity" is composed of the constantly stratified layers of our abiding past—our heritage or "effective-history"—through which we appropriate a possible future.[14]

The stratified, malleable, and incessantly renewable self-externalized traces of all that we have been—our heritage or "effective-history"—is that out of which a conceivable future can possibly arise. In this regard, theoretic work is a constant and ongoing reflexivity aimed at the critical appropriation of the possibilities of our "effective-history" and focused on the clarity and cogency of our own conceptions. For, in order not to be reduced to "quelque chose d'extérieur au sérieux de la vie" [something external to the seriousness of life],[15] theory has to solidly anchor itself in, and arise from, the specificity of a heritage in the pressing concerns of life.

II

The first chapter, "Heritage and Its Transmission: A Reading of Frantz Fanon," is an exploration of the question of heritage as it occurs in Fanon. Supplemented by Hans-Georg Gadamer's conception of "effective-history"—worked out in *Truth and Method*—this initial chapter presents a reading of Fanon focused on the enigmatic heritage of Westernized Africa.

Chapter 2, "Identity and Race in the Black Experience: Reflections on W. E. B. Du Bois," and chapter 3, "Master and Slave: African American Slave Narratives and Hegel's Dialectic of Recognition," are focused on Du Bois, and the question of race in the concrete and lived self-formation of African American identity,[16] and an examination of slave narratives in light of Hegel's dialectical conception of recognition. In both chapters, the theme of heritage will be engaged in terms of a concrete interpretive exploration of the lived experience documented in slave narratives and in Du Bois's efforts and recommendations regarding African American identity.

Chapters 4 and 5, respectively, are focused on the question of African identity and the contemporary scene in African philosophy. Chapter 4, "Africa and Identity: Kwame Anthony Appiah and the Politics of Philosophy," presents a critical reading of Appiah's book *In My Father's House* and explores the consequences, political and theoretic, of the views he advocates.[17] Chapter 5, "African Philosophy? Looking behind the Question," is a reading of the question of African philosophy in terms of the contemporary needs of the continent. In both chapters, formulations in African philosophy are critically gauged in terms of the heritage that, in my view, we Africans need to project into the future in order to ameliorate the situation of our blighted continent.[18]

Chapter 6, "The Heritage of the Idea: Violence, Counterviolence, and the Negated," is, as the title indicates, an exploration of the legacy of metaphysically legitimating violence that we owe to the European tradition of philosophy. Relying on a destructive reading of key figures in this powerful tradition, the chapter will show European speculative thought to be a brazen "colonial witness,"[19] complicit in the imperious adventure of European colonial self-globalization.

The conclusion, in view of all of the above, will present a synoptically concise enunciation of the stance that informs the text as a whole. This stance, on the level of theory, required by our contemporary situation—labeled "the postcolonial sensibility"—is that of

> the formerly colonized, the oppressed, that of the under-developed who struggle for more justice and equality. From this point of view, the validity of an interpretation is tied to the validity of a struggle: of its justice and of its justness. Here, I affirm the methodological importance of praxis for hermeneutics, praxis understood in the sense of an action tending towards the qualitative transformation of life, [for] in a given situation, it is praxis which assigns to hermeneutics its place and its development. Praxis unlatches the hermeneutic process and gives it an orientation. Hermeneutics, in its turn, offers praxis a cultural self-identity, necessary for ideological combat.[20]

In terms of this stance, "theory is not added to practice as a luxurious supplement, it enlightens practice which, in turn, provokes it in a dialectical manner."[21] In other words, it is not a question of "writ[ing] books. That may be good or bad."[22] It is a "concern" aimed at a critical linkage of "understanding with a project of change,"[23] in view of what is possible in and out of our concrete situation, in and out of our lived heritage, that is, our "effective-history."

I have labeled this "point of view" the postcolonial sensibility:[24] a stance philosophically focused on the critique of the grounding assumptions of imperious European modernity and its enduring dregs and striving toward, on the political level, a shared and truly postcolonial global heritage. This stance takes its hybridity seriously and strives to make this medley (out of which it originates) the ground for the hopes, aspirations, and possibilities of the future.

Conditions change from generation to generation, and accordingly, theoretic reflection has to reflexively, and on an ongoing basis, reorient itself to the needs of praxis, on its own terms and from within the lived condition of flux and change: the incessantly mutating permanence of the present. For, as Hannah Arendt tells us, relying on René Char, action has value and "completion only in the minds that inherit and question it."[25] It is toward such a theoretic interrogation of our shared heritage that this study is aimed.

1

Heritage and Its Transmission: A Reading of Frantz Fanon

Broadly speaking, and looking exclusively from a philosopher's vantage point, the specific manner in which Africa, south of the Sahara, was affected by the experience of enslavement and colonialism can be described as a systematic undermining of its multiple and diverse heritage, the differing foundations of its cultural, spiritual, sapiential, political, and economic traditions. Arab Africa, north of the Sahara, was colonized and subjected to economic exploitation or reduced, when not directly colonized, to the inferior status of a political dependency. Its heritage (i.e., identity), however, embalmed and preserved in Islam, was never seriously threatened or in any fundamental way undermined. To this day, it challenges the hegemony of the West in all aspects of life, confronting it concretely in politically sustained fundamentalist movements aimed at a frozen, archaic, and arcane past.

As Dr. Hasan Turabi, an eminent Sudanese Islamic thinker and spiritual leader, informs us, all that is needed is to go back to the "unitarian principle" of Islam and to the example of the Prophet.[1] Thus, for the Arab north, for better or for worse, the thread of its cultural heritage persists. This is not so for the rest of black Africa. For the heritage of the continent is not limited to, or coterminous with, the heritage of Islam.

As is well known, the question of heritage is what Kwame Nkrumah in 1964 made the centerpiece of his philosophic reflections in *Conscienism.*[2] While I find myself in agreement, on the whole, with much of Paulin J. Hountondji's critique of this text, it seems to me rather cavalier and thoughtless to dismiss the basic theme of heritage that animates Nkrumah's thinking by saying, as Hountondji does, that "the Africanness of our philosophy will not necessarily reside in the themes but will depend above all on the geographical origin of those who produce it and their intellectual coming together."[3] But if it is not "themes" that define the "Africanness" of our philosophy, what does? Around what will the "intellectual coming together" of those who "produce it" occur? For philosophers (African or otherwise) are human beings and, like everybody else, congregate or come "together" around issues, concerns, or celebrations focused on a common theme and/or a cluster of themes. Indeed, Hountondji is well aware of this as it pertains to the development and practice of modern European philosophy.[4] What, then, of African philosophy? Is Hountondji's geographic and nonthematic conception a different "special" type of philosophy for Africa? Is he vying with the ethnographic conception, whose critique he initiated, for a "special-status philosophy" for Africa? Leaving these questions for the reader to mull over, this chapter will engage the theme of heritage as it pertains to black Africa.

The basic task is to reflect on the way our fractured de facto heritage affects us. The aim is to explore the way these effects can possibly be utilized to overcome the explicitly felt and lived enigma of our heritage.[5] In this, the work of Frantz Fanon, supplemented by Hans-Georg Gadamer's notion of "effective-history," will be the guiding thread of my efforts.[6]

A focused reading of Fanon,[7] in the way he understands the question of heritage, is thus the basic concern of this initial chapter. I will begin by posing the question (section I) and go on to explore Fanon's thinking (sections II and III) that makes for a critical grasp of our heritage in its transmission.

I

As the noted African philosopher from Cameroon, Marcien Towa, has appropriately observed,

> Normally, the identity of a people or a civilization is not a problem; it goes without saying. Each people displays certain characteristic traits which differentiate it, more or less, from others. Some of these particular traits may become the object of derision or mockery . . . just as other traits may be admired. . . . The situation becomes qualitatively different, [however,] when the consciousness of self, of this particularity, becomes an *obsession,* invades the most intimate depths of subjectivity, inspiring all literary production and taking on the dimensions of a veritable ideology.[8]

This "obsession," furthermore, pertains directly and in the first place to Westernized Africa. To confirm this observation one need only take stock of the fact that all the great intellectual productions of this Africa—the poetry of Négritude (Césaire, Senghor, Diop); Nkrumah's notion of an "African personality" and his efforts in *Consciencism;* and the productions of African (francophone and anglophone) literature by Kane, Sembène, Oyono, Ngũgi, Achebe, Soyinka—in differing ways focus on the colonial impact and the in-between identity of Westernized Africa that is a residual effect of this impact.[9]

This (non)identity, this in-between, is the ambiguity of our heritage. For we are the ones—in one way or another—who live and have experienced this "ambiguous adventure" and feel, in the very depth of our being, the unnerving experience of being two in one, Europe and non-Europe.[10] This anguish of "being two"[11] is what forces on us—Hountondji notwithstanding—the question of heritage as the thematic of the "Africanness" of our philosophic reflections. For as Fanon has described it, "There is a zone of non-being, a region extraordinarily sterile and arid, a plundered declivity essentially stark-barren, from where an authentic resurgence can take birth. In the majority of cases, the Black person does not have the benefit of realizing this descent into a veritable Hell."[12] This "zone de non-être"— that the Westernized African dwells in when he or she realizes the perplexing anxiety of the "being two" of his or her lived actuality and heritage—is an unsettling, threatened, and threatening region. For Westernized Africa, this "zone of nonbeing" is what makes the question of heritage acute, for it puts into question the countenance and actuality of our future. It makes problematic the being of our existence and denies us the luxury of taking it for granted.

In and out of this "zone de non-être" Fanon concretely engages the question of heritage. The Islamic fundamentalists, in their arcane piety, are sheltered from the anguish of "cette descente aux véritables Enfers" [realizing this descent into a veritable Hell]. They exist in an either/or: European modernity or obsolete Islamic Africa! This "zone de non-être," this concretely lived in-between, does not exist for Dr. Turabi. Hountondji, too, to the extent that he is snug and restful in the certitudes of European thought—Althusierian Marxism!—is insensitive to this "zone de non-être," the restless space that Fanon knew so well. Inversely, and for inverse reasons, Turabi and Hountondji each assuage and nullify the other's anxiety.

For the Westernized African, on the other hand, who is forced to focus on the truth of his or her Westernization, the question of heritage is a question of "nonbeing." Anguished, between a desecrated frozen past and an arrogant and domineering Europe, this gap is the living space of Westernized African existence. Thus, the question: Who are we, we who are directly implicated by this question and that which it renders questionable? Or as Ferdinand Oyono has put it, "Brother, what are we? What are we black men who are called French?"[13]

For as Fanon sarcastically puts it, "The 'bush savage' is not envisaged here."[14] This is precisely because the question of heritage is concerned with the Westernized generations of the present who descend, or have sprung forth, from those "in whom fear has been cunningly instilled, who have been taught to have an inferiority complex, to tremble, kneel, despair, and behave like flunkeys."[15] To be sure, since Aimé Césaire first wrote these words in 1955, the political geography of Africa has undergone tremendous change. To some extent "fear" and "despair" have been surmounted, and Westernized Africa has stood firm with the "bush savage" in ending the era of direct colonial rule.

But, for the most part, we still "tremble" and quake at the sight and sound of our former colonizers and are, in every respect, dependent on them. The "bush savage," on the other hand, and the centuries-old heritage that persists and has endured in his or her being, are and continue to be suppressed:

Repressed, persecuted, betrayed by some social groups who were in league with the colonialists, African culture [i.e., the "bush savage"] survived all the storms, taking refuge in the village, in the forests and in the spirit of the generations who were victims of colonialism. Like the seed which long awaits conditions favorable to germination in order to assure the survival of the species and its development, the culture[s] of African peoples flourish . . . again today, across the continent, in struggles for national liberation.[16]

Indeed, during the period of the "struggles for national liberation," when colonialism was confronted—in various and differing historical settings—both politically and militarily, during these glorious moments of modern African history, Westernized Africa stood firm, took on positions of leadership, and made the political demands of the "bush savage" its fighting slogans.[17] This was a moment in modern African history when the enigma of our heritage was momentarily dissolved in our actual participation in the making of our own history. But, as future historians will note, this was a very short-lived period, a fleeting moment, of modern African history.

Paradoxically, with the attainment of independence, the quaking resumes. Old habits and habituations die hard! Just as the West rules over us (Westernized Africans) from the inside by inhabiting the interior space—the very mold of our lived existence—in like manner, we conduct or transmit this dominion, slightly indigenized, and impose the West—mediated through our own lived existence— on the "bush savage." Or, as Sembène Ousmane has pointedly observed, "We want[ed] the ex-occupier's place? We have it. . . . Yet what change is there really in general or in particular? The colonialist is stronger, more powerful than ever before, hidden inside us, here in this very place. He promises . . . the left-overs . . . if we behave ourselves."[18] And, indeed, we do not find it difficult to behave! For behavior has to do with habituation, with "vices" and "virtues," learned and acquired through conditioning and mimicry.[19] For we are still addicted to the "Greco-Latin" soma,[20] the vices and "virtues" of imperial Euro-America and all that they oblige/force us to be. This is the negative possibility of the nationalist parties that Fanon warned would come to pass with the attainment of formal independence: the defeat—through and in victory—that defines contemporary postcolonial Africa. Thus, the schism in African existence, the enduring mark/brand of the colonial experience, between "us" and "them"—the Others, that is, the "bush savage"—is conserved, sustained, perpetuated, and incessantly produced, as a matter of course, into the future. How, then, does one overcome this schism?

This is for us the question of the inquirer, the question of heritage, for "the very asking of this question is an entity's mode of Being."[21] Indeed, this guilty question encapsulates the sum and substance of Westernized Africa's literary, political, and philosophic self-"obsession."[22] The "bush savage," on the other hand, endures an existence that is inert, impotent, and excluded from the lived actuality of the contemporary world. Having taken the "ex-occupier's place," Westernized

Africa parrots the gestures and attitudes of imperious Europe, the *mère coloniale* (colonial mother),[23] that nurtured it to adulthood. In lording it over the "bush savage," it does so as a good understudy, with borrowed and affected gestures. What, then, is the character of this guilty question?

In asking about our heritage, we cannot but ask this question from within a perspective that is explicitly informed by the political actuality of the way our existence has been made manifest and rendered actual in a world dominated by the West. As Africanist historian Basil Davidson has noted, up to the closing years of the nineteenth century, "most Africans in Western-educated groups . . . held to the liberal Victorian vision of civilization kindling its light from one new nation to the next, drawing each within its blessed fold, long after the local facts depicted a very different prospect."[24] Having accepted the self-proclaimed and self-serving European civilizing fantasy, in 1901, for example, Angolans living in Lisbon published a protest against Portuguese misrule of their country. The outrage, in the eyes of these Angolans—that is, Westernized Africans—was not that "Portugal had conquered Angola centuries earlier" but, rather, that, "the people [still] remain brutalized, as in their former" precolonial condition.[25] The outrage in this outrage is that the Westernized Africans have made the purported self-righteousness of Europe's colonial enterprise their own.

Thus snared and implicated in their own colonial domination, marked and branded by their own hands, Westernized Africans, as a distinct section—not European and not quite indigenous—of formerly colonized Africa, are guilty beings. It is this in-betweenness, the acceding to Europe's civilizing fantasy in loathing recognition of being African, that grounds the lack of security, the self-effacing *xala* (impotence), that "becomes an obsession,"[26] dominates our lived concrete predispositions, and in its negativity—when cognized as such—prods and provokes our thinking. For as Fanon puts it, "Those who condemn this exacerbated passion strangely forget that their own psyche, their own selves are commodiously sheltered behind a French or German culture which has given full proof of its existence and which is uncontested."[27] The question we face, then, is one of existence. But this is not a facile or empty question about anxiety and the dullness of life. Quite to the contrary, it is a deadly earnest concern with our existence that puts into question the whole edifice responsible for the formation of this very existence. Located, between actuality and its actualization, in the lived "being-in-the-world" of Westernized Africa, it calls into question the very ground of its origin—the ground of the colonial project, that is, its own lived existence. For as Edward W. Said has noted,

What distinguishes earlier empires, like the Roman or the Spanish or the Arab, from the modern empires, of which the British and French were the great ones in the nineteenth century, is the fact that the latter ones are systematic enterprises, constantly reinvested. They're not simply arriving in a country, looting it and then leaving when the loot is exhausted. [M]odern empire requires . . . an idea of service, an idea of sacrifice, an idea of redemption. Out of this you get these great, massively reinforced notions of, for example, in the case of France, the *"mission civilisatrice."* That we're not there to benefit ourselves, we're there for the sake of the natives.[28]

The Westernized African or the "ex-'native,' "[29] who has not "bénefice de réaliser cette descente aux véritable Enfers" [benefited from realizing this descent into a veritable Hell],[30] is indeed the actualized embodiment of these "massively reinforced notions." Having soaked up and internalized "the colonizer's perspective," such a person is "incapable of doing anything without" the colonizer's assent, endorsement, tutelage, and/or approval.[31] Such a person is degraded into being the marionette or parrot of preordained schemes—stages of history? stages of economic growth? and so on—and cannot properly engage in exploring fresh historical possibilities.[32]

Such a person does not have a way of grasping the sense of things—that is, the eventuations of his or her own lived, existent history—beyond or outside of colonial and/or Eurocentric schematizations. For his or her lived awareness of Self and Other is grounded on "acknowledging [for whatever reason] that one was low on the hierarchy of achieved wisdom,"[33] on accepting "the death and burial of" one's own "local cultural originality"[34] as a given need of world history—that is, of progress, development, or the general improvement of human life on earth and so on.

What then happens when such a being, a nonentity, comes to an awareness—to a lived realization of his or her own existent actuality—as a nonbeing? This is the moment of the question of heritage and "of combat."[35] It is a coming to consciousness, felt as a "veritable Hell," for it is experienced in the way the inmates of Kafka's "penal colony" live and/or endure their punishment.[36] It is in and out of such an awareness that Fanon calls us, in his understanding of how we are to relate to our heritage and its transmission.

Thus, to ask about our heritage is to ask, Are we a multitude of spineless carbon copies, humanized apes, whose "way out"[37] is the mimicry that inflicts on the "bush savage" the very suffering—slightly indigenized—of our own lived (de)formation? Are we the embodiments of a "universal-humanoid abstraction"[38] that, cringing, can aspire to nothing more, or less, than "a servile imitation"[39] of Western humanity? For heritage is to a people what character is to an individual, and as an ancient oracle reminds us, "Character for man is destiny."[40]

My purpose, in this initial chapter, is limited to this reflexive question regarding our fractured heritage, a deracination in which we ourselves are implicated. It is an attempt to seriously consider Heraclitus's oracular truth, to the extent that we hear it, we, who are inculpated in the fractured character/heritage "hidden within us,"[41] which—from within—closes off our own lived and concrete possibilities.

Having preliminarily shown that the question of heritage originates in an awareness of our fractured identity as a "zone de non-être," let us now examine the way the question was posed for us—by Fanon—in and out of the lived ambient of the

African anticolonial struggle. For "we are always subject to the effects of effective-history. It determines in advance both what seems to us worth inquiring about and what will appear as an object of investigation."[42] Taking this hermeneutical truth as our point of departure, let us explore Fanon's conception of how we are to engage our heritage in order to further expand on the propitious gains that constitute its actuality. In other words, this study itself—as a moment of reflexivity— is a theoretic "effect" interior to the abiding "effective-history" it reflects on.

II

In the first sentence of the fourth chapter of his seminal work, *The Wretched of the Earth,* written from within the concrete ambient of the African liberation struggle, Fanon states, "Each generation must out of a relative opacity discover its mission, fulfill it or betray it."[43] This stern sentence—this call—by an African militant being consumed by leukemia is, on the one hand, rather clear and simple. Each generation has a mission; this mission is to be fulfilled or betrayed. To this extent it is clear and simple.

But does each generation have a mission? And if it does, where does this mission originate or come from? What is Fanon calling us to? It is here that the complexities of Fanon's stern message to future generations, to us, who are to read his words, are located. What, then, are these complexities? Let us try to untangle them by way of an example, a detour.

In the small hours of the morning, a muezzin calls out, "Allah Ua Akbar. . . ." Who heeds the call? To the nonpracticing Muslim, to a Christian or an atheist, resident of the city or village in which the muezzin practices this religious vocation, the call goes unheard and unanswered. Or rather, what is heard is a disturbance of early morning sleep and the requisite response is to close the window shutters tighter or cover one's head snugly under the bed covers. Or, alternatively, one could imagine a tourist, a foreigner, listening to the melodic undulations of the muezzin's voice and experiencing it on an aesthetic level as an unexpected delight of visiting an "exotic" place which the tourist bureau failed to mention. Or again, one could imagine a city, suffering from Muslim-Christian strife (Beirut during the Lebanese civil war) in which the call is heard alternatively as an appeal to steadfastness and/or as a threat that conjures up images of kamikaze Muslim fighters.

Who hears the call? Those who have already made the faith and its call the destiny of their lives—the faithful. They hear it because it resonates and harmonizes, within them, with their chosen faith/fate. It is—in their hearing—what it proclaims: the truth that calls them to their fate and thus to their own-most-self, the *Mesgid* (mosque), the congregation, the faith.

The call is the summons of conscience, which calls and is heard only to the extent that one feels fated and called, feels responsible.[44] It is a call that comes from within a world that the caller and the called inhabit and by which they are saturated—formed in their individuality—and exist in as human beings. To "fulfill or betray it," to be responsive to or not responsive to and thus responsible for and to the call, is to own up to one's own-most possibilities, or fail to do so, within the ambient of a present and lived heritage. Thus, to hear the call is to turn "freedom into destiny."[45]

The muezzin's call is heard by those in whom it resonates. It is not an objective declaration. It is, rather, within this resonance that the muezzin rehearses his lived and concrete calling, his vocation. If one is a Christian, a nonpracticing nominal Muslim, an atheist, a vacationer, or a Muslim or Christian partisan (or bystander) in a city or town riven by religious conflict, the call of the muezzin is alternatively heard or not heard, aesthetically enjoyed or tolerated, felt as a threat or a summons to arms, depending on one's situation, one's concrete stand or "stance" in life.[46] Indeed, this is what Fanon calls us to, to an awareness that the lived experiences that constitute our fractured heritage are the ground or stand of our existence.

In our detour we have noted that the muezzin and the faithful, the caller and the called, partake of a living heritage, a concrete ethical-religious whole that constitutes their specific individuality and existence. But Fanon calls from within a lived fracture, an open wound; his call, unlike the muezzin's, does not rest on given and established normative structures. His call originates from a lived experience of fracture, a concrete absence, a "gap between actuality and ideality."[47]

But is this not the fractured heritage inaugurated by colonialism and perpetuated by neocolonialism which the African liberation struggle has, thus far, failed to overcome? From within this heritage of fracture, to respond means to reclaim those moments, in modern African history, when the different levels of urban Westernized Africa turned to the rural—peasant and nomad, that is, the "bush savage"—mass of indigenous folk and with them engaged in struggle to build a new world and concretely grasp a possibility of history.[48] This is the moment, in modern African history, when the enigma of our heritage was momentarily dissolved, when, fleetingly, the fracture of our existence was overcome.

As noted above, this lost possibility—defeated through and in victory—that defines postcolonial Africa is the ground from which arises the anguished question of heritage.[49] Towa points out, in synchrony with Fanon, this "zone de non-être": "The anguished conscience of our identity is in reality the consciousness of the loss of identity under the dissolving action of external forces which we have not succeeded in controlling."[50] Thus, to properly respond to Fanon's call is to overcome the ground of this malaise—in effect, to reclaim and consolidate that fleeting moment in modern African history, when the enigma of our heritage was momentarily dissolved, to reclaim and anew consolidate that moment in modern African history—defeated in and through victory—which makes worthy of questioning the question of our heritage. This is what Fanon calls us to.

III

Now to reclaim is to repeat—and this always and of necessity—out of a different horizon, or a different vista, within the same horizon. As Gadamer points out,

> The horizon is the range of vision that includes everything that can be seen from a particular vantage point. Applying this to the thinking mind, we speak of narrowness of horizon, of the possible expansion of horizon, of the opening of new horizons etc. The word has been used in philosophy . . . to characterise the way in which thought is tied to its finite determination, and . . . the range of vision.[51]

He continues, "The horizon of the past, out of which all human life lives and which exists in the form of tradition [i.e., heritage], is always in motion. It is not historical consciousness that first sets the surrounding horizon in motion. But in it this motion becomes aware of itself."[52] In its lived existence, "each generation" sees for itself its own-most possibilities out of the concerns of its own horizon.

In Fanon's formulation, a "generation" is not a numerical aggregate; rather it is those who respond to a "mission." This "mission," discovered out of a "relative opacity," is not a given fact. It is that which is heard from within a heritage and disclosed as a possibility in one's horizon. For the "motion" of a heritage "becomes aware of itself" only in concrete individuals and as the horizon of their lived self-awareness. Understood in this manner, "each generation" is encompassed within a horizon that harbors all that has been and presents various vistas and possibilities as one moves toward it.

Fanon, an "ex-'native' "[53] writing from the lived horizon of the African liberation struggle, calls us, those who like him straddle two worlds, replete with ongoing and systemic contradictions. But he is not concerned only with "ex-'natives,' " as such, but with all those who have a stake in the lived "effective-history" he calls from, all those who can hear his call. For it is in the living and thinking of those who embrace it that a heritage—an "effective-history"—"becomes aware of itself," just as the call of the muezzin is what it proclaims in the hearing of the faithful.

Thus, Fanon is not calling for "revolutionary socialism" or the placing of "the colonized people under the command of the peasant class."[54] Neither is he writing exclusively for "ex-'natives,' " for he calls Europe to "stop playing the stupid game of Sleeping Beauty" and shoulder her responsibilities.[55] To be sure, as Sartre has dramatically observed, "For the fathers, we alone were the speakers; the sons [Fanon and the "ex-'natives' " he writes for] no longer even consider us as valid intermediaries: we [Europeans] are the objects of their speeches."[56] But surely Sartre exaggerates for effect in emphasizing the spectacular reversal that Europe suffered in the rebellion of "the sons" of "the fathers" it humiliated! For, as Sartre knew quite well, Fanon directly addressed himself to and was concerned with "la minorité européenne d'Algérie" [the European minority of Algeria].[57]

Fanon's call is directed to "ex-'natives' " and to the generations of Europeans and *colons* who experience their colonizing and imperial heritage as an impediment, dead weight, a constricting horizon. It is directed to the radical elements in Europe and her colonies—today her ex-colonies, the whites of South Africa, for example—that are opposed to the colonial heritage even as they unwillingly benefit from it. It is directed to the "colonizer who refuses,"[58] who having distanced and severed his or her ties to the colonial heritage is not susceptible to "those prejudices that are of a particular and limited nature"[59] and, in being so, composes the colonial horizon. In such a person these prejudices have decomposed and "die[d] away," have lost their effectiveness, and in their stead "those [prejudices] that bring about genuine understanding emerge clearly as such."[60] For the "colonizer who refuses" in refusal—in the very act of refusing—radically changes the directionality of his or her horizon of life possibilities.

In this choice he or she becomes open to the "effects" of a different "effective-history." In refusing, such a person negates—for whatever reason—his or her self-understanding, within the colonial horizon, in terms of which he or she had lived life up to that point.[61] In other words, "those [prejudices] that bring genuine understanding" are the very ones that negate the colonial heritage and embrace—with all of its risks and possibilities—the emergent horizon of the heritage of the struggle.[62]

To be sure there are those, like Albert Camus, who declare that they are "neither victims nor executioners."[63] And to this one can respond with Sartre:

> A fine sight . . . the believers in non-violence, saying that they are neither executioners nor victims. Very well then; if you're not victims when the government which you've voted for, when the army in which your younger brothers are serving without hesitation or remorse have undertaken race murder, you are, without a shadow of a doubt, executioners. And if you choose to be victims . . . your passivity serves only to place you in the ranks of the oppressors.[64]

Unlike Camus, the "colonizer who refuses" has already become part of a new heritage in formation. To be sure, Fanon's statement that "hundreds and hundreds of European men and women" have given "constant support" to the resistance could be seen, after the event, as hyperbolic.[65] Even so, this exaggeration itself is evidence of the openness of Fanon's call. For, as he tells us, "The colonized person who writes for his people when utilizing the past must do so with the intention of opening the future, as an invitation to action, and as a ground for hope."[66] The "past" here refers to the "effective-history" of the colonized. But it is also inclusive of those aspects or "effects" of the colonizer's history that are not highlighted in the colonial horizon but are embraced by the anticolonial struggle (i.e., the discourse on rights and liberties, women's liberation, the slogans of the workers' movement, etc.).[67] For the horizon of the struggle is a medley of all its elements. And the possibility of the freedom of the colonized and neocolonized necessarily—in the very process of its actualization—has to come to terms with the de facto reality of a globalized Europe.

As Cheikh Hamidou Kane—a "colonized person who writes for his people," in Fanon's formulation—has noted, "We have not had the same past, you [Europe] and ourselves [Africa], but we shall have, strictly, the same future. The era of separate destinies has elapsed. In this sense, the end of the world has indeed come for each of us, because no one can any longer live by the simple carrying out of what he himself is."[68] It is the possibility of this "future," grounded in a shared "effective-history" forcibly inaugurated by Europe's colonial globalization and the ensuing demise of the "era of separate destinies" which the "ex-'native' " embodies, that grounds Fanon's call. If it is focused on the "ex-'native,' " as Sartre claims, this is so because, unlike the descendant of colonizers who has embraced the cause of the colonized or neocolonized, or the European radical—Sartre, for example—the "ex-'native' " lives (in the very fiber of his or her being) the necessity of this shared horizon. It is not, for him or her, a radical political option, a "fight in the name of theoretical justice."[69]

The "ex-'native,' " the ethnic rural African, the colon who refuses, and the European radical in joint effort and struggle institute not "separate destinies" but a future cultivated out of the "effective-history" that constitutes the horizon of the struggle. This is what Fanon calls us to: "Cet oxygéne qui invente et dispose une nouvelle humanité" [This oxygen which invents and makes possible a new humanity].[70] And what is this "oxygen"? It is the medley of diverse histories and joint efforts that constitutes the ethos of the struggle and concretely prefigures the possibility of inaugurating a new humanity.[71]

But what exactly is the character of this new humanity to which Fanon calls us—descendants of colonizers and colonized—in aspiring to overcome the Eurocentric humanism of the past? This "new humanity could arise only through the creative praxis of the colonized."[72] But perhaps it may come not only from the praxis of the colonized, for "we, Algerians [i.e., non-Europeans] want to discover the human being behind the colonizer."[73] "The settler is not simply the person that must be killed. Many members of the mass of colonialists reveal themselves to be much, much nearer to the national struggle than certain sons of the nation. The barriers of blood and race-prejudice are broken on both sides":[74] In breaking the "barriers of blood and race-prejudice" and in the very act of doing so, concurrently, the struggle institutes, culled and cultivated out of the "effective-history" that is actualizing it, a heritage in formation. It creates, or makes out of itself, a new ethos—a tradition or heritage—of the daily life that constitutes the struggle. And this new horizon is not confined within the colonial territories but has a boomerang "effect" on the people—the ordinary citizens—of the colonizing power. As Fanon tells us,

Certain settlers do not join in the criminal hysteria. . . . Such men, who before were included without distinction and indiscriminately in the monolithic mass of the foreigner's presence, actually go so far as to condemn the colonial war. The scandal explodes when the prototypes of this division . . . go over to the enemy, become Negroes or Arabs, and accept suffering, torture, and death.

Such examples disarm the general hatred that the native feels toward the foreign settlement. The native surrounds these few men with warm affection, and tends by a kind of emotional over-valuation to place absolute confidence in them. In the mother country, once looked upon as a blood-thirsty and implacable stepmother, many voices are raised, some those of prominent citizens, in condemnation of the policy of war that their government is following, advising that the national will of the colonized people should be taken into consideration. Certain soldiers desert from the colonialist ranks; others explicitly refuse to fight against the people's liberty and go to prison for the sake of the right of that people to independence and self-government.[75]

In sum, the question of heritage that, as we saw, originates in the felt anguish of the Westernized African—that is, Fanon's call, which comes out of a lived "zone de non-être"—is addressed to, and possibly heeded by, not only the "ex-'native' " but all those whose coming together (i.e., the fusion of horizons) made possible and opened up the horizon within which the downfall of colonialism (i.e., the "effective-history" of imperious Europe) was actualized.

As noted earlier, this heritage was defeated in and through victory.[76] For Fanon, what is at stake in this defeat concerns both sides of the equation: colonizer and colonized. For "Europe, for ourselves and for humanity," Fanon writes, "we must make a new skin, develop a new thinking, try to put afoot a new human being."[77] This "new humanism both for itself and for others [that is] prefigured in the objectives and methods" of the struggle is a possibility only to the extent that the sublated "primitive Manicheism" of the colonial era does not re-emerge.[78] Only to the extent that we manage "to make a new skin [and] develop a new thinking" is this a possibility. For a heritage, as Gadamer tells us, is not transmitted "by nature because of the inertia of what once existed"; it must be sustained, "affirmed, [and] embraced" to maintain itself in and as the present.[79]

The heritage of the struggle beyond the defeat of colonialism, this "new humanity," "pour soi et pour les autres,"[80] this is what Fanon calls us to. This, furthermore, is not a cultural-historical egoism "opposed to *homo barbarus*."[81] It is an Other-directed openness, not "an already established interpretation of nature, history, world, and the ground of the world."[82] It is an open-ended project of a humanity, in process, that finds itself in joint struggles. Fanon is the muezzin of this project. To hear his call is to respond and be responsible for and to this struggle—the concrete effort to overcome the fracture of our heritage—in and out of the horizon of the present.

2

Identity and Race in the Black Experience:
Reflections on W. E. B. Du Bois

In the second chapter of *In My Father's House,* entitled "The Illusion of Race," Kwame Anthony Appiah claims that W. E. B. Du Bois's understanding of race in "The Conservation of Races" (1897), and his view of African Americans as a distinct people with a message to give the world, are clear examples of what Jean-Paul Sartre has, in an analogous context, referred to as "antiracist racism." As Appiah puts it,

> What is essential [for Du Bois] is the thought that Negroes, by virtue of their socio-historical community, can achieve, through common action, worthwhile ends that will not otherwise be achieved. On the face of it, then, Du Bois's strategy here is the antithesis of a classic dialectic in reaction to prejudice. The thesis in this dialectic — which Du Bois reports as the American Negro's attempt to "minimize race distinctions" — is the denial of difference. Du Bois's antithesis is the acceptance of difference along with a claim that each group has its part to play, that the white and Negro races are related not as superior to inferior but as complementaries; the Negro message is, with the white one, part of the message of humankind. *What he [Du Bois] espouses is what Sartre once called — in negritude — an "antiracist racism."*[1]

What I would like to do in this chapter is challenge Appiah's assertion that Du Bois in "The Conservation of Races" espouses what Sartre has characterized as "antiracist racism." This, in my view, is an aspect of Appiah's position that has not been properly examined by some of those who have queried his critique of Du Bois.[2] By way of remedying this shortfall, I will look at Du Bois's text and examine what it means to say that it is a case of "antiracist racism." I will then glance at the original context in which Sartre makes the above remark and explore Frantz Fanon's response to this remark.

My intent is to show that Du Bois, in contrast to Appiah and in accord with Fanon, takes seriously the actuality and weight of lived experience in the way it constitutes the historicity and heritage — in an ongoing manner — of black life. This, then, is a reading of Du Bois, by way of Fanon, focused on Du Bois's efforts to sustain and reclaim the heritage of human "existence in black" on this side of the Atlantic.[3]

I

In "The Conservation of Races," a talk Du Bois gave at the founding of the American Negro Academy in 1897, he poses the question "What, then, is race?" and answers, "It is a vast family of human beings, generally of common blood and language, always of common history, traditions and impulses, who are both voluntarily and involuntarily striving together for the accomplishment of certain more or less vividly conceived ideals of life."[4] Starting from and based on this understanding of race, Du Bois goes on to assert that American Negroes should not try to "minimize race distinctions"[5] but live up to the challenge of the message of the Negro people—yet to be delivered to the world—and that this delivery depends on their own efforts, which must be grounded in organization, solidarity, and unity centered on themselves.[6] As he puts it,

> Let us not deceive ourselves at our situation in this country. Weighted with a heritage of moral iniquity from our past history, hard pressed in the economic world by foreign immigrants and native prejudice, hated here, despised there and pitied everywhere; our one haven of refuge is ourselves, and but one means of advance, our own *belief* in our great destiny, our own implicit trust in our ability and worth.[7]

For Du Bois, if "self-obliteration" is not to be "the highest end to which Negro blood dare aspire,"[8] then "for the development of Negro genius, of Negro literature and art, of Negro spirit, only Negroes bound and welded together, Negroes inspired by one vast ideal, can work out in its fullness the great message we have for humanity."[9] This furthermore can be achieved only if we are "fearlessly"[10] critical of our own motives and actions and, in every respect in harmony with other races, are unsparing in our efforts to improve and change our situation. As he puts it, we have a "vast work of self-reformation to do,"[11] and this needs earnest and hard toil. It is Du Bois's view, furthermore, that it is not only Negroes but all the differing races of humanity who have messages to deliver. In each case, the differing groupings of humanity render their message to the world only to the extent that they nurture a deeply felt "belief" in their own particular humanity—their historical and cultural existence.

The then newly established American Negro Academy was to be a vehicle for this great undertaking, a center grounded on the "belief" in, and the hoped-for actualization of, the historical possibilities of African American existence. It was to be "a clearinghouse" for all the "products of the Negro mind"[12] during a period of time when the general public was firmly convinced that not much, if anything, could be expected from "the Negro mind." Du Bois concludes his talk by suggesting six propositions as the "Academy Creed." The first two state,

1. We believe that the Negro people, as a race have a contribution to make to civilization and humanity, which no other race can make.
2. We believe it the duty of the Americans of Negro descent, as a body, to maintain their race identity until this mission of the Negro people is accomplished, and the *ideal of human brotherhood has become a practical possibility.*[13]

"The Conservation of Races" is a reflection on the adverse situation of African Americans in a predominantly racist society. Its rhetorical force is aimed at awakening the conscience and consciousness of those most concerned and afflicted by this situation. And it articulates a program of action confined within the historical space required to achieve "the ideal of human brotherhood."

To this extent Du Bois's remarks are limited and speak to the exigencies of the time, as he saw them, and do not concern themselves with the question of race as such. "The Conservation of Races" calls on those whose identity and humanity have been the object of racist persecution to actively pull themselves together and, instead of "minimizing race distinctions,"[14] defy the challenge to their humanity by forming organizations centered on themselves.[15] The core focus of Du Bois's text is the concrete self-transformative effect of political struggle that molds the specific histories of differing peoples. Du Bois is concerned with mobilizing the human resources of the Negro community so that this community can act in self-defense and in so doing—in this very act—cultivate and assert the very humanity that the dominant racist society is negating.

Writing from within and out of the lived struggle of African American life—a situation whose main protagonists were/are the descendants of former slaves under the dominion of the descendants of former masters—Du Bois challenges the racist status quo by engaging in the formation of black institutions (the American Negro Academy in 1897, the National Association for the Advancement of Colored People in 1909, etc.) and insisting on the safeguarding of black identity. This, furthermore, he recommends as a sensible course of action, till such time when "the ideal of human brotherhood has become a practical possibility."[16] On this point Du Bois is in agreement with Sartre's notion that human liberation is, ultimately, aimed at doing away with all particularisms. His concern is, thus, not to defend and maintain some Negro essence—as such—but to help create and cultivate the conditions for black freedom.

Far from endorsing or espousing an "antiracist racism" as Appiah suggests, Du Bois is a committed intellectual whose efforts are aimed at actualizing as a "practical possibility" the "ideal of human brotherhood." But as an organic intellectual, concretely involved in the political struggles of his people, he is well aware that this ultimate ideal—"human brotherhood"—can be achieved only by the actualized self-determination, in all its aspects, of those who have been violently excluded from it. For "brotherhood" presupposes recognition, at least in principle, of a shared humanity in terms of which it can possibly be established.

For a position that could be described as an "antiracist racism" we can cite Léopold Senghor, who maintains that "emotion is completely Negro as reason is Greek [i.e., white]."[17] Now, in fairness to Sartre, it has to be said that his formulation is an apt description of Senghor's position, for Senghorian Négritude is indeed grounded on essentialized notions of blackness and whiteness as racial types, and this is indeed an "antiracist racism." But Du Bois is not Senghor!

Du Bois does not parcel out essential and essentialized human attributes—reason and emotion—along racial lines. He is not concerned with a Negro essence. His claim is not that there are pure types that need to be preserved.[18] Quite to the contrary, his claim is that, given racist oppression, those of us thus oppressed need to, in an organized manner, confront this affront to our humanity. In this respect, his position is analogous to Aimé Césaire's conception of Négritude as "a concrete rather than abstract coming to consciousness" of our specific humanity.[19] As is well known, Césaire's Négritude is concerned not with the essence of blackness but with the lived political actuality of black existence.

All peoples, for Du Bois, in the particularity of their existence are implicated in the actualization of their history. He, thus, calls on the African American community—his people—to actively recognize this ontological truth of our lived and shared human situatedness. The message of each people is not an essence, inscribed in race, but the result of effort and struggle: hence the need for organization and the cultivation of the Negro people in intellectual and cultural productions. For history is the realm not of individuals but of cultural and historical totalities or human communities.[20] Or as Hans-Georg Gadamer points out, commenting on the concrete existence of individuals within sociohistorical communities,

> Every single individual that raises himself out of his natural being to the spiritual finds in the language, customs and institutions of his people a pre-given body of material which, as in learning to speak, he has to make his own. Thus every individual is always engaged in the process of *Bildung* and in getting beyond his naturalness, inasmuch as the world into which he is growing is one that is humanly constituted through language and custom. Hegel emphasises that a people gives itself its existence in its world. It works out from itself and thus exteriorises what it is in itself.[21]

The term *Bildung,* as Gadamer tells us, signifies growth "out of [an] inner process of formation and cultivation . . . in a constant state of further continued *Bildung.*"[22] Analogous to the Greek notion of *physis,* "Bildung has no goal outside of itself."[23] It is its own end. It signifies an ongoing process of self-formation through which "a people gives itself its existence in its world."

Now if we look at the above, in terms of Du Bois's view that African Americans have a "great message . . . for humanity,"[24] what it means is that it is to the exigencies of their own lived existence that African Americans must be equal—individually and collectively—in engaging the historic tasks of their existence as a people. For it is out of themselves that they are to "exteriorize" what it is that they are as a people. And this is not a peculiarity of African American existence, as such, but an ontological truth of our shared humanness.

Du Bois takes culture and history seriously and understands that the struggle against racism, in its hopes and aspirations, is aimed not at self-obliteration but at the articulation of the specific difference that constitutes the oppressed as people and which is reclaimed—in the process of struggle—beyond the negativity and negation of racism. To say, as Appiah does, that Du Bois's "acceptance of [the] difference" that constitutes distinctly African American existence is a case of "antiracist racism"[25] is to claim, at least tacitly, that we owe our culture—our particular humanness—to racism. In effect, if not in intention, this is what Appiah maintains.

While it is true that, in its origins, African American history and culture came to be as a result of the slave trade and slavery, it is not true that this culture, once established, is no more than a result of white racism. For the blues, jazz, African American literature, and so on, are not the mere by-products of racism but, rather, the effects and secretions of the humanity of the human, of those whose history has been an ongoing and incessant struggle against this odious phenomenon. Or, in Gadamer's formulation, "A people gives itself its existence. . . . It works out from itself and thus exteriorises what it is in itself." Just as Emmanuel Levinas has pointedly observed that "we do not owe Judaism to anti-[S]emitism,"[26] in like manner one needs to cue Appiah that we do not owe the vivacious actuality of African American life to racism.

It is the cultivation and sustenance of this life—against all odds—that concerns Du Bois in "The Conservation of Races." What matters for Du Bois is that the "sociohistorical community" of the descendants of former slaves come to recognize "through common [political] action" the worth, valor, and dignity of its own humanity.[27] For the heritage of this humanity—won and secured through blood and tears—can survive and be perpetuated into the future only if the historical community of those whose suffering and struggle produced it maintains itself as a community, a people, that is, a race—in the language of Du Bois's times.

Let us now turn to the originative context in which Sartre formulates the notion of "antiracist racism" that Appiah utilizes against Du Bois. In other words, let us quickly glance at the source of Appiah's flawed critique of Du Bois.

II

In *Black Orpheus,* which was originally the introduction to Senghor's *Anthologie de la nouvelle poésie négre et malgache de langue française,* Sartre thinks of the situation of the black person, in a racist society, as being analogous to that of the proletariat. For Sartre, Négritude is the negativity, the "antiracist racism,"[28] that is destined to be sublated and disappear in the universal dialectic of human liberation. Just as the proletariat is the extreme and negative pole of capitalist society that liberates itself by negating its own conditions of existence and of bourgeois society as a whole, Négritude is, analogously, the self-negating extreme negativity created by a racist world. In this reading of Négritude, which Appiah shares with Sartre's *Black Orpheus,* we owe the cultural specificity of black people to the negativity of racism![29] Fanon, in his critique of *Black Orpheus,* as we shall soon see, pointedly observes that beyond this negativity, and more important than it, there is a black identity to be lived.

Sartre, in taking the struggle of the proletariat as his model for understanding Négritude, fails to see the key and fundamental *dis*analogy between the two cases. The proletariat struggles to transform the relations of production, expropriate the capitalist class, and, in so doing, appropriate for society as a whole the wealth—material and cultural—produced under capitalism. In this acrimonious conflict—the schematic Sartre utilizes in looking at Négritude—the protagonists in struggle are engaged in contesting the fruits of a shared cultural and historical heritage within the ambient of a single social formation. In other words, the class struggle occurs on the concrete ground of a shared "existential spatiality" and lived history.[30]

The proletariat is concerned with negating this "existential spatiality" within which it exists as an oppressed class. In struggling to negate itself as an oppressed class, its efforts are focused on appropriating—and, thus, transforming into public wealth—the publicly produced and privately consumed material and cultural opulence of capitalist society. Négritude, on the other hand, in its negativity, is aimed at reclaiming, not negating, the violently suppressed "being-in-the-world" or "existential spatiality" of black life.

The struggle is aimed at revalidating the cultural and historical ontic actuality of a people as a specific way of disclosing existence. In other words, humankind is history or historical, always within specific temporal communities articulated in a language and a culture that constitute its ontic specificity or "existential spatiality." It is always within the ambient of a specific "existential spatiality" that a human being is human. Each person stands in the light and shadow of being or existence made possible by the cultural and historical existential space that nurtures his or her life, and, in turn, this lived "existential spatiality" is interior to and is sustained by the community of life that it shelters and, thus, makes possible.

Seen in this light, the poetic longing of Négritude is aimed at negating not itself but, rather, the conditions of life that fix it as a "human thing."[31] It is aimed at reclaiming concretely a black "existential spatiality." For it is the negation of this lived space—this historical existence—that constitutes the experience of enslavement.

In contrast to Sartre in *Black Orpheus,* Fanon is concerned with the lived actuality and cultural particularity of the black person "who is driven to discover the meaning of black identity" and is aware that "what is often called the black soul" is itself a construction of European or white culture.[32] Fanon writes,

> The crippled veteran of the pacific war says to my brother, "Resign yourself to your color the way I got used to my stump; we're both accident victims."
> Nevertheless with all of my strength I refuse this amputation. I feel in myself a soul as immense as the world, truly a soul as deep as the deepest of rivers, my chest has the power of infinite expansion. I a Don am counseled the humility of the infirm.[33]

Fanon establishes a link between the "stump" of the handicapped person as a form of identity and blackness as an identity. If, then, my blackness as a black person is merely or nothing more than the mark of my accidental and catastrophic encounter with European/white domination, and if it is itself a white construct, what then of my identity? As noted in the first section of this chapter, Appiah's critique of Du Bois in endorsing Sartre's formulation is precisely this: that Du Bois accepts, in a positive guise, the racist position he combats.

In contradistinction to Appiah, and in accord with Du Bois, Fanon's answer to this question, the question of black identity, points to the "existential spatiality" reclaimed by the struggle to overcome European or white domination as a black identity, always in process, that constitutes itself in confronting domination. It describes the various stances and configurations of being black that are the concrete self-formation of a black identity, which is not merely a "stump," a black unchanging essence, the positive residue—in reverse—of white racism.[34]

For in discarding the notion of blackness as nothing more than the "stump" of the black person's negative encounter with racism, Fanon does not ignore but recognizes the lived actuality of the blackness of the black person. Against Sartre's reduction of the "being-in-the-world"[35] or the "existential spatiality" of black existence to nothing more than the self-destructive and negative moment of the universal dialectic of human liberation,[36] Fanon writes, "Without a Negro past, without a Negro future," it is "impossible for me to live my Negrohood."[37] But what exactly is this Negrohood *(nègrerie)*?

In parting company with Sartre, Fanon, utilizing Hegel's master-slave dialectic, points to the formative struggle of African American life. The focal moment of the master-slave dialectic, for Hegel, is the struggle of the slave, mediated by labor and in absolute fear of death, through which enslavement is overcome. As Fanon puts it,

> The former slave needs a challenge to his humanity, he wants a conflict, a riot. But it is too late: The French Negro [West Africa, Martinique] is doomed to bite himself and just to bite. I say "the French Negro," for the American Negro is cast in a different play. In the United States, the Negro battles and is battled. There are laws that, little by little, are invalidated under the Constitution. There are other laws that forbid certain forms of discrimination. And we can be sure that nothing is going to be given free. There is war, there are defeats, truces, [and] victories.[38]

In distancing himself from Sartre, Fanon does not end up by departing from "the historical world"[39] and endorsing some kind of fixed Negro or black essence à la

Senghor. Rather, as should be clear from the above quotation, he points to "defeats, truces, [and] victories" as that which constitutes our lived "Negrohood," the specific aspect of humanity embodied in us.

Du Bois's "The Conservation of Races," written as it is in the midst of struggle and conflict—of the descendants of former slaves and former masters—is a call to add to our "victories," minimize the effects of our "defeats," and hence work toward the realization of the "ideal of human brotherhood." Du Bois and Fanon, contra Appiah, clearly recognize that the way to the "ideal of human brotherhood" requires the sublation of race oppression by the reciprocal recognition of the worth and value of the various human groupings—or races, in the language of Du Bois's time—that constitute the concrete actuality of humankind as a whole. For beyond the *uni*verse of racism lies the horizon of our shared *multi*verse humanity.

To argue, as Appiah does, at the end of the twentieth century, that Du Bois's position is an "antiracist racism" is to fail to see that the antiracist struggle is not, and never has been, an effort at self-obliteration but an effort at reclaiming the humanity—instanced in specific cultures and histories—of those whose humanness has been and is presently the object of racist persecution. In other words, the effort is to make de jure our lived de facto multiverse humanity. This requires, among other things, the concrete reclaiming of the suppressed "verse" of our shared being as humans. This was the central task that Du Bois assigned himself in his political work as an organic Negro/African American intellectual.

III

Understood in this light, "The Conservation of Races" is not about race as such. It is, rather, a call to those on this side of the Atlantic—who suffer racial segregation and oppression—to enhance, via concrete political struggle, their own modality of existence. But what might this be? This is what Du Bois refers to as "the great message we have for humanity."[40]

Human life, in contradistinction to the actuality of inert objects or animal life, is a being-in-the-world that does not have a peculiar essence per se. All that it has is a constant possibility "to be" *(Zu-sein)*[41] and, in being, to actualize itself as a constantly actualizable possibility. The specific way in which human beings are "in" the world—given this ontological interpretation or conception of what they are—is actualized by the cultural, historical, and concrete political self-formation of a community of people. As I have argued in the first part of this chapter, Du Bois—from within the lived ambient of his community and in the political language of his "times"—calls for the preservation of the African American modality of life in the face of racist oppression and persecution.

Viewed in this light—in the way Du Bois understood it—the African American struggle for equal citizenship, the civil rights movement, for example, was not and is not merely a struggle for political equality. More importantly, it was and is a crucial moment in the ongoing and fluid self-formation of African American identity/existence. For in the very struggle to end segregation and blatant bigotry, African Americans concretely and simultaneously mold, transform, and discover themselves and, in so doing, establish the actuality of their freedom and the limits of the tolerable henceforth. As Dr. Martin Luther King has noted,

> Many of the Negroes who joined the [Montgomery] protest did not expect it to succeed. When asked why, they usually gave one of these answers: "I didn't expect Negroes to stick to it," or "I never thought we Negroes had the nerve," or "I thought the pressure from the white folks would kill it before it got started."
>
> In other words, our nonviolent protest in Montgomery is important because it is demonstrating to the Negro, North and South, that many of the stereotypes he has held about himself and other Negroes are not valid. Montgomery has broken the spell and is ushering in concrete manifestations of the thinking and action of the new Negro.[42]

In other words, the movement "is demonstrating to the Negro, North and South, that many of the stereotypes [of] himself are not valid." A stereotype is a typecast, a fixed identity. In the passage quoted above, Dr. King affirms that the movement transforms the fixed identity in which African Americans were forced to live their existence during segregation and ushers "in concrete manifestations of the . . . new Negro."

In an earlier time, as Booker T. Washington tells us, "after the coming of freedom," a cultural manifestation on "which practically all the people were agreed" was the need to change names. In other words, "there was a feeling that" slave names such as "Hatcher's John [were] not the proper title by which to denote a freeman; and so in many cases 'John Hatcher' was changed to 'John S. Lincoln' or 'John S. Sherman,' the initial 'S' standing for no name, it being simply a part of what the coloured man proudly called his 'entitles.'"[43] It is from a feeling of the undignified and fixed status of slavery and in claiming their own humanity that the formerly enslaved name themselves. This naming, "what the coloured man proudly called his 'entitles,'" is an act of dignifying and actualizing one's freedom within an all-enclosing ambient, a heritage in formation. It is an act of self-creation. Indeed, as Gadamer has noted, "A people gives itself its existence. . . . It works out of itself . . . what it is in itself."[44] And as Fanon points out, in an analogous context, "This [self-]creation owes nothing of its legitimacy to any supernatural power";[45] it is the consolidation of actualized freedom. It is, in other words, the summation of the struggle to achieve this very freedom.

Taking a parallel stance, Rosa Parks, when asked "why she refused to move to the rear" of the bus, stated, "It was a matter of dignity; I could not have faced myself and my people if I had moved."[46] In refusal, Parks reclaimed, within the context of her moment of time, her human "entitles," that first jubilation that marked the end of slavery!

In like manner, the founding document of the Organization of Afro-American

Unity, Malcolm X's last political initiative, states, in no uncertain terms, that the self-appellation of a people is a central component of the process of its liberation. Thus, after a systematic rejection of the term *Negro* and of its "blunt and unde-ceptive" derivatives, *nigra* and *nigger*,[47] the document goes on to state that "we accept the use of Afro-American, African, and Black man in reference to persons of African heritage. To every other part of mankind goes this measure of just respect. We do not desire more nor shall we accept less."[48] In naming themselves, in the refusal and discipline of the movement, in every effort aimed at reclaiming humanity, the formerly enslaved carve out and reclaim, at each phase of the strug-gle, the heritage of their freedom. Each effort aimed at freedom or enacted within the ambient of a limited freedom and aimed at enhancing this already achieved freedom situates a specific or concrete engagement within one's heritage: the "effective-history" of one's existence. The actuality of a heritage is, then, the lived sedimentation, the layering of the self-formation that constitutes a specific history.

To point to the "defeats, truces, [and] victories" that constitute our lived her-itage, as Fanon does, is to assert that we are beings who constitute and exist within the limits of a given situation and do so in a constant and ongoing process of self-transformation. For looked at from the perspective of the enslaved, the identity of the black person who is forced to live in segregation is actualized freedom. On the other hand, after Rosa Parks, segregation—and the heritage it enforced—can only be seen as a momentary defeat of our black humanity.

Each victory once achieved is surpassed and subsequently appears as a momen-tary setback. As Du Bois points out, what matters in all of this is the refusal of "servile imitation" and the insistence on "unswervingly follow[ing] Negro ideals."[49] But what might these "Negro ideals" be? Are they the ideals for which, since the days of slavery, African Americans have struggled and died, ideals for-mulated out of their own needs and aspirations, whose achievement has been punc-tuated by "defeats, truces, [and] victories"? These ideals are the ways in which a community understands itself, names itself, and sees its place in the world. Indeed, Du Bois's attachment—as a leading African American intellectual—to the "ideal of human brotherhood," in the midst of racist oppression, is itself a concrete man-ifestation of the character of these ideals.

The various self-ascriptions of life that constitute the identity of a community at any one point in time are never static but always in the process of sustaining themselves and, thus, always in change. When two or more such ascriptions are in use during the same period of time in the historical life of a community, they may indicate differing formulations of future possibilities or ideals that the community articulates through its leading voices. Dr. King, for example, used the term "'Negro' when he referred to the African American community[;] on the other hand Malcolm X despised the term 'Negro' as a self-designation. He preferred 'African,' 'black,' and 'Afro-American.' "[50] These differing "preferences" reflect specific political choices—by Dr. King and Malcolm X—that reflect differing readings and interpretations of the future possibilities of the community they spoke for. In like manner, when individual African Americans take on an Arabic and/or African name the intent is not to distance themselves but to affirm a specific identity or reading of the lived actuality and future possibility of their African American community. In other words, as human beings, we are those beings that constantly project their future from within the bounds of constituted communities, which are such precisely because they are the totality of our shared projects.

Given the above, then, our identities are neither static nor singular but in a constant process of self-elaboration, always start from an "effective-history," and are formulated in terms of possibilities that are grasped in view of a hoped-for future. In this regard, Malcolm X's preference for the term *African,* for example, points to his efforts at seeing the African American situation in light of the then-prevalent dynamic developments on the African continent. Dr. King's use of the term *Negro,* on the other hand, has the effect of valorizing, and thus overcoming, the negativity affixed on this ascription. Similarly, the term *Négritude,* in the use that Aimé Césaire makes of it, has the effect of positively appropriating the term *négre* and overcoming the negativity imposed on it; for Césaire (unlike Senghor's essentialism), Négritude has nothing to do with reason or emotion but is "a concrete rather than an abstract coming to consciousness" of who we are as human beings in the context of a concrete history.[51]

If Appiah sees this as an "antiracist racism," this is so precisely because he thinks that the antiracist effort is aimed at obliterating all difference. In effect, what this does is universalize the culture of racism and disregard the strivings of those who suffer it. For "our spiritual strivings"—the specific actualization of our humanity—in all of its triumphs and failings, is what constitutes the "message" of our history and concrete existence.[52]

It is concrete history and its exigencies that Du Bois is concerned with in "The Conservation of Races"; and, analogously, in Fanon's critique of Sartre, his focus is the "Negrohood" of African American existence and its possibilities. For behind the "veil,"[53] mutilated and obstructed by it, is the historicity of black existence which seeks to resurrect itself into a concrete historical freedom: "Some day the Awakening will come, when the pent-up vigor of ten million souls shall sweep irresistibly towards the Goal, out of the Valley of the Shadow of Death, where all that makes life worth living—Liberty, Justice, and Right—is marked 'For White People Only.'"[54]

3

Master and Slave: African American Slave Narratives and G. W. F. Hegel's Dialectic of Recognition

In the introduction to *The History of Mary Prince a West Indian Slave*, Moira Ferguson states that G. W. F. "Hegel argues, the moment of revolution comes when the slave recognizes that his or her primary identity lies with the other slaves, and as a result withdraws both labour and recognition. At this point when the slave no longer sees his or her identity as necessarily mediated through the master, then not only is the slave not a slave but the master is not a master."[1] In point of fact Hegel does not say any such thing! To be sure, the master-slave dialectic is a central moment of the *Phenomenology of Spirit,* but Ferguson's paraphrase owes nothing to Hegel's dialectical conception of mastery and slavery. In fact, in a note for the above, Ferguson does not cite—as she should—the paragraphs in Hegel's text that we must assume she is elucidating; rather, she refers to the first chapter of Alexandre Kojève's famous *Introduction to the Reading of Hegel.*[2]

Now, in the first chapter of his book Kojève explores, very creatively, the dialectic that brings into play the key idea of recognition. This movement of the dialectic is directly tied to the marginality of the surpassed master and the achieved autonomy and freedom of the former slave consciousness, which has endured and gone through the master-slave dialectic. In other words, Kojève is engaged in showing how "it is indeed the originally dependent, serving, and slavish Consciousness that in the end realizes and reveals the ideal of autonomous Self-Consciousness and is thus its 'truth.'"[3] As Kojève shows, in no uncertain terms, this is achieved in the confrontational movement and lived traversing of the master-slave dialectic. Ferguson, then, misreads not only Hegel but also Kojève, the authority she cites for the legitimacy of her interpretation.

By focusing on Hegel, and not Kojève, in this chapter I will engage the master-slave dialectic, and in so doing I will show how slave narratives can be used to elucidate the idea of recognition that is the central component of Hegel's text and, conversely, utilize Hegel to show how in struggle the enslaved reclaim and constitute, in freedom, their own concrete humanity. Contra Ferguson, it is not the withdrawal of "labour and recognition" but the consummation—that is, the complete traversal—of the lived interimplicative dialectic of the master and the slave that necessarily ends in the marginality of the master and the autonomy and freedom of the formerly enslaved consciousness.

The importance of this point lies in the fact that freedom, for Hegel, is an achievement grounded in the recognition—by the consciousness of the formerly enslaved—that going through and surpassing the dialectic of its own self-constitution through the master—that is, this process itself—is the lived and concrete actuality of freedom. Short of this, for Hegel, the "overcoming" of a master—an empirical one—is not the overcoming of mastery per se.[4] For what is required is the transcending of the very idea of mastery and slavery as such.

What is at stake in all of the above, then, is our understanding of the character of the freedom of the formerly enslaved. In this regard the radical difference that one finds in the attitude—toward slavery—of an Olaudah Equiano (or Gustavus Vassa, the African) and a Frederick Douglass can serve as a good example, in the concrete, of what needs to be rescued from Ferguson's interpretation.

I

As is well known, for Hegel the experiential self-constitution of consciousness, which he refers to as "the Science of the experience of consciousness,"[5] is a dialectically interimplicative process that has itself as its own measure and criteria. This is what Joseph L. Navickas points to as Hegel's discovery of consciousness's "self-mediating process."[6] Hegel's presentation is, furthermore, cumulative and necessarily presuppositional; thus, in order to focus on the notion of recognition—which is our main concern—it is necessary to look at the basic structure of the work as a whole, focused on the sections that precede and follow the segment with which we are concerned.

Consciousness in its immediacy, and in the process of overcoming this immediacy, manifests interconnected levels of awareness, each of which gives way to the other as a more adequate level of knowledge. "Sense-certainty" is the immediate consciousness simply sensing the immediacy of the external as "this," "here," and "now." This immediacy, in actualizing itself, gives way to perception, and, on this level, consciousness perceives the "external-to-itself" as a particular object, "the thing." In turn this level gives way to "the understanding," and, on this level, consciousness understands for the first time that the objects of its knowledge are forces and laws. Thus, it comes to pass that—in the object—it has been observing only itself, perceiving and internalizing the object, and that the understanding—which is the self-actualization and unfolding of consciousness thus far—"experiences only itself."[7]

Now consciousness is certain of itself only insofar as it negates that which is Other than itself. It proves to itself that it is the essential reality by negating or overcoming all that is not itself. It asserts and shapes itself in negation.

Thus, it comes to pass that consciousness becomes aware that the external is independent of it and that it itself is dependent on the external for its own certainty of self. Consciousness here finds itself at an impasse because it recognizes itself as the ordering principle of the object and yet does not see itself in the object. In recognizing itself as the ordering principle, consciousness has now become—for the first time—aware of itself as self-consciousness. Reality is, for it, itself understanding itself—and this is its truth: "But now there has arisen what did not emerge in these previous relationships, viz. a certainty which is identical with its truth; for the certainty is to itself its own object, and consciousness is to itself the truth. In this there is indeed an otherness; that is to say, consciousness makes a distinction, but one which at the same time is for consciousness *not* a distinction."[8] What follows is an analysis of self-consciousness in its movement of coming to know itself in actualizing the insight—which it gained on the level of the understanding—that it itself is its own object. As Hegel puts it, "Self-consciousness exists in and for itself when, and by the fact that, it so exists for another; that is, it exists only in being acknowledged. The Notion of this its duplication embraces many and varied meanings. . . . The detailed exposition of the Notion of this spiritual unity in its duplication will present us with the process of Recognition."[9] The "process of Recognition" is, then, the concrete duplication of self-consciousness and, in this, the arduous, dire, and necessarily uncompromising struggle of self-consciousness to impose itself on the other—that is, an Other self-consciousness—the way this Other imposes itself on the object. Recognition then arises from the duplication of self-consciousness whereby each sees the Other as the locus of its actualization in being recognized and, thus, each denies the Other what the Other asserts for itself. Thus, recognition is the essential result of the master-slave dialectic. For self-consciousness needs an Other (i.e., like itself) to recognize it so as to go beyond its dependence on the object. Thus, *"self-consciousness achieves its satisfaction only in another self-consciousness."*[10] But what is this satisfaction? It is the assured certainty of self-consciousness in the truth of what it is.

We have now reached the crucial stage of the master-slave dialectic and the struggle for recognition. But before going on to see the relevance of all of the above to the truth expressed in slave narratives and, conversely, the way these narratives concretely substantiate Hegel's speculative insights into the character of human freedom, it is necessary to make a detour and look more closely at the method through which Hegel explores the unfolding of spirit in the actuality of self-consciousness. In other words, we need to scrutinize more closely the ebb and flow of what Navickas refers to as "the self-mediating process," that is, the actuality of the all-important dialectic.

II

The *Phenomenology of Spirit,* Hegel tells us, expounds "an example" of the applicability of his method to "a more concrete object."[11] What method does Hegel have in mind?

Hitherto philosophy had not found its method; it regarded with envy the systematic structure of mathematics and . . . borrowed it or had recourse to the method of [the] sciences which are only amalgams of given material, empirical propositions and thoughts—or even resorted to a crude rejection of all method. However, the exposition of what alone can be the true method of philosophical science falls within the treatment of logic itself; for the method is the consciousness of the form of the inner self-movement of the content of logic.[12]

In other words, the *Science of Logic* enunciates the proper method of philosophy, which is "the inner self-movement of the content" itself. In this regard, the *Phenomenology of Spirit* is an application of this method in considering the diverse "forms of consciousness" in their various morphological developments and determinations. The form of consciousness, says Hegel, in "realizing itself at the same time resolves itself, has for its result its own negation—and so passes into a higher form."[13] The reliability of this method, which for Hegel is the "only true method," lies in the fact that it is not distinct from, but one with, its object.[14]

In explaining the significance of Hegel's method, Hans-Georg Gadamer writes that "the method of dialectic must guarantee that the explication of the train of thought is not arbitrary. [O]n the contrary, the advance from one thought to the next, from one form of knowing to the next must derive from an immanent necessity. In the *Phenomenology of Spirit* that advance is played out in a most intricate fashion."[15] Or as Jean Hypolite explains, "The dialectic is the life of the object and dialectical thought is in no way an abstract categorization. Every living relation has its own particular structure which must be conceptualized as such."[16] The merit of Hegel's method, therefore, lies in the fact that it does not impute to its object anything external; rather, it closely follows the self-unfolding "from one form of knowing to the next" and develops its movement "from an immanent necessity" in the "thought-object" itself: "No expositions can be accepted as scientifically valid which do not pursue the course of this method and do not conform to its simple rhythm, for this is the course of the subject matter itself."[17] This, furthermore, is done by grasping the negative: "That which enables the notion to advance itself . . . the . . . *negative* which it possesses within itself; it is this which constitutes the genuine dialectical element."[18] The "negative" is the principle of movement; or, as Hegel puts it, "Only when the manifold terms have been driven to the point of contradiction do they become active and lively towards one another receiving in contradiction the negativity which is the indwelling pulsation of self-movement and spontaneous activity."[19] Indeed, as Gadamer points out in *Truth and Method,* in contrast to the leveled and uniform conception of experience to be found in the natural sciences and the historico-critical method, Hegel retains the "historicality" of experience in his conception of the negative. The "negativity" of experience is the central moment through which the dialectical unfolding of thought and its object is activated and realized.[20] It should thus be clear that in the *Phenomenology of Spirit* Hegel is not engaged in the mere transposition—that is, crude application—of the categories developed in the *Science of Logic;* rather, he is engaged in the concrete, dialectical, and lived self-unfolding of spirit in the actuality of consciousness and self-consciousness.

Indeed, in the quick glance that we took of this process (section I) we have been able to see how the "self-mediating process" of consciousness actually works by an internal process of negation. In keeping with all of the above, then, in looking at slave narratives what I intend to do is to show how, in these narratives, there is a dialectic at play that parallels Hegel's exposition and is aimed at the attainment of human dignity and freedom, that is, recognition.

The challenge will not be to force the significations of Hegel's dialectical formulations onto slave narratives but to see how these narratives—in what they say—affirm the dialectical insights of Hegel's speculative reflections. And, in turn, we shall also see that Hegel's reflections on the character of recognition substantiate—in all essentials—the sufferings, struggles, and strivings documented in slave narratives.

III

Frederick Douglass's *Narrative* is the self-conscious expression of a formerly enslaved person (or self-consciousness) addressed to a public, specifically those influenced by the political work of the abolitionist movement and possessed of the somber recognition of the necessity for the complete eradication of mastery and slavery.[21] The *Narrative* is a document of the double process through which a human being is broken into slavery and overcomes this very process. In chapter ten, the central chapter of the *Narrative,* Douglass states, "You have seen how a man was made a slave; you shall see how a slave was made a man."[22] The actualization and reversal of the double process through which one is enslaved and, in resistance, reclaims humanity are our central concern in looking at Douglass's narrative.

Before becoming a slave Douglass was "a man." But because he was born into slavery, one might ask, What period of his life precedes his enslavement? Douglass gives us an answer to this question in the very first chapter of his *Narrative.* He was born of a white father (his first master) to a slave mother, and his early years of adolescence were spent in the care of his maternal grandmother, "on the outskirts of the plantation, where she was put to raise the children of the younger women."[23] This was indeed a very economic use of aged slave labor, for a child is a hindrance to a young working slave mother from the point of view of her master.

This common practice, however, of placing young slave children and infants in the "care of an old [slave] woman, too old for field work,"[24] must be seen as a period of time in the life of a person born into slavery in which the infant or young child lives at some "distance" from the brutality of enslavement and within the human embrace of an aged benevolent guardian and/or grandparent. The frugal

use of aged slave labor had thus—given the brutal political economy of slavery—
the unintended effect of negating the brutality of the system at the very inception
of the personalities of those enslaved.

Thus, using Douglass's conceptualization, we can say that in this period of his
life Douglass—and any other young slave in a similar situation—was not a "slave
in fact" but only "a slave in form."[25] For enslavement, like freedom (contra
Rousseau), is not a natural endowment but a lived historico-existential actuality.
Human beings are not born slaves, they are made slaves, that is, they are enslaved
or broken into slavery. Thus, Douglass's adolescence precedes his enslavement
properly speaking. It is out of this relatively "edifying" and familial milieu that
Douglass is plunged into an awareness of his enslaved situation.

As he tells us in the first chapter of his narrative, his mother died when he was
circa seven years old, and soon thereafter he witnessed the "horrible exhibition"
of his Aunt Hester's flogging. This event Douglass describes as "the blood-stained
gate, the entrance to the hell of slavery, through which I was made to pass."[26] Once
Douglass crossed through the "blood-stained gate" into the world of enslavement,
his life and the lives of his fellow slaves were constituted by an ongoing process
of methodical brutality and the systematic diminution of their humanity.

How so? Every event in a slave's life is directly tied to the fact of his or her
enslavement and his or her subordinate position. Over and above this, if a particular aspect of the slaves' being goes against the grain of this subordination by, for
instance, being "a constant offence to their mistress"[27] (i.e., the plight of mulatto
slaves, for example), to that extent the slaves are physically, psychologically, and
emotionally tormented and made to suffer—precisely because they cannot be
allowed to think themselves above, or different from, their enslaved status.

For in being what they are—slaves—they are not only chattel but a constant
reminder of the need for brutality in the maintenance of the bestial relation of the
master to the slave. To be sure, in all of this, the feelings of the slave are not to be
considered, for the slave is supposed to be a nonhuman entity. The slaves' sorrows,
human feelings, relations, familial ties, and so on count for nothing,[28] and it is only
in the "joy" of going to the "Great Farm House"[29] or the dehumanized fighting
over "the relative goodness"[30] of differing masters that the slave is allowed a sense
of self or humanity. This is allowed, furthermore, only to the extent that it concretely cements the slave more closely to his or her enslavement.

For to quarrel over "the relative goodness" of differing masters is "to think that
the greatness of their masters is transferable to them."[31] But even in this the suppressed humanity of the enslaved seeps through, for, as Douglass points out, in
their songs on their way to the "Great Farm House," for example, the slaves
expressed "at once the highest joy and the deepest sadness."[32] And anytime this
sadness—the felt and lived consciousness of the loss of one's humanity—was
asserted in anything more than song, open conflict ensued. This is what the story
of Demby elucidates:

Mr. Gore [an overseer] once undertook to whip one of Colonel Lloyd's slaves, by the name of Demby. He had given Demby but a few stripes, when, to get rid of the scourging, he ran and plunged himself into a creek, and stood there at the depth of his shoulders, refusing to come out. Mr. Gore told him that he would give him three calls, and that, if he did not come out at the third call, he would shoot him. The first call was given. Demby made no response, but stood his ground. The second and third calls were given with the same result. Mr. Gore then, without consultation or deliberation with any one, not even giving Demby an additional call, raised his musket to his face, taking deadly aim at his standing victim, and in an instant poor Demby was no more.[33]

What does Demby's courage give us to understand, in terms of Hegel's master-slave dialectic? Demby like Douglass has passed through "the blood-stained gate, the entrance to the hell of slavery." Thus, in refusing to be flogged he is asserting against Gore, the concrete master, his will as a human being and repudiating the fear and terror that first inaugurated his enslavement—his terrifying passage through "the blood-stained gate" which must be perpetuated and maintained to keep the enslaved in their abject condition. For the slave is a slave only to the extent that he or she is forced to internalize his or her existence as chattel. Only in groveling at the sight and sound of the master does the slave remain a slave.

Thus, strictly speaking, Demby does respond to Mr. Gore's calls by refusing to comply. And in this refusal Mr. Gore is forced to recognize that Demby is a being endowed with a free will, that is, a self-consciousness assured in itself. Demby's refusal is a contestation from within an already established situation of mastery and slavery—that is, the master-slave dialectic. This confrontation, which ends with Demby's death, results in an "abstract negation, not the negation coming from consciousness, which supersedes in such a way as to preserve."[34] For the development of the dialectic of recognition requires a negation of freedom that preserves the life that it negates.

As Hegel points out, to seek the other's death is necessarily to risk one's own life. For what is true of one self-consciousness is also true of the other, in reverse. At this point one could object: Demby's confrontation with Gore is occurring within an already established master-slave relation, thus the concrete master, Gore, does not really risk his life. This is an accurate observation as it pertains to the particular case of Demby and Gore in its specific particularity. But, as the slave breaker Mr. Covey discovered—much to his dismay—in confronting Douglass, certain circumstances can create a situation such that the assured mastery over the enslaved can be openly put into question and challenged.[35] For, as Hegel points out, "The other is an *immediate* consciousness entangled in a variety of relationships, and it must regard its otherness as a pure being-for-self or as an absolute negation."[36]

At any point self-consciousness can put into question the "variety of relationships" in which it is "entangled" and which constitute it as what it is: dependent or free. Indeed, this is what Demby does in refusal and in so doing is willing to sacrifice his life in bondage for the possibility of a free existence. In refusing to comply and in being willing to die, Demby repudiates the fear and terror that constitute his enslavement and sees himself as "a pure being-for-self." Gore kills Demby because, in refusal, Demby reclaims or recognizes the truth of his being, that is, freedom.

In this regard the story Mary Prince tells of a "slave called old Daniel" is quite revealing:

> Poor Daniel was lame in the hip, and could not keep up with the rest of the slaves; and our master would order him to be stripped and laid down on the ground, and have him beaten with a rod of rough briar till his skin was quite red and raw. He would then call for a bucket of salt, and fling upon the raw flesh till the man writhed on the ground like a worm, and screamed aloud with agony. This poor man's wounds never healed, and I have often seen them full of maggots, which increased his torments to an intolerable degree. He was *an object of pity and terror* to the whole gang of slaves, and *in his wretched case we saw, each of us, our own lot.*[37]

For a slave, to revolt or refuse—as Demby does—is to reject the internalized "pity and terror" through which the slave master holds the enslaved groveling in their bondage. To refuse or revolt is to challenge that initial moment of enslavement that the enslaved is forced to accept—on an ongoing basis—in fear and terror. In this regard, the suffering of "old Daniel" is not gratuitous; indeed, given the brutal political economy of slavery it is the very cement that keeps the system intact.

For the enslaved has to constantly be dehumanized, and cowering has to be his or her mode of existence: and this not only in fear of brute physical force but also in recognition of his or her helpless situation in being—in every respect—a thing, a piece of property.[38] It is all of this that Demby contests in staking his life for his freedom. For, as Hegel points out,

> Thus the relation of the two self-conscious individuals is such that they prove themselves and each other through a life-and-death struggle. They must engage in this struggle, for they must raise their certainty of being *for themselves* to truth, both in the case of the other and in their own case. And it is only through staking one's life that freedom is won; only thus is it proved that for self-consciousness, its essential being is not [just] being, not the *immediate* form in which it appears, not its submergence in the expanse of life, but rather that there is nothing present in it which could not be regarded as a vanishing moment, that it is only pure *being-for-self.*[39]

In the confrontation with Gore, Demby is killed, but he does not die a slave but a free person. For in refusal Demby shows to himself and to his adversary that "there is nothing present" in him "which could not be regarded as a vanishing moment" and that the only thing that counts is his "pure *being-for-self*," that is, his freedom. Indeed, it is precisely in recognition of this that Gore kills him.

Let us now look at a situation in which the revolting slave is not murdered but manages—as a result of being "entangled in a variety of relationships"—to stand his ground and survive.[40] Let us look at the moment in the life of Frederick Douglass in which he reclaims his humanity. Douglass writes,

> I was called to go and rub, curry, and feed, the horses. I obeyed, and was glad to obey. But whilst thus engaged, whilst in the act of throwing down some blades from the loft, Mr. Covey [a notorious slave breaker] entered the stable with a long rope; and just as I was half out of the loft, he caught hold of my legs, and was about tying me. As soon as I found what he was up to, I gave a sudden spring, and as I did so, he holding to my legs, I was brought sprawling on the stable floor. Mr. Covey seemed now to think he had me, and could do what he pleased; but at this moment—from whence came the spirit I don't know—I resolved to fight; and, suiting my action to the resolution, I seized Covey hard by the throat; and as I did so, I rose. He holding on to me, and I to him. My resistance was so entirely unexpected, that Covey seemed taken all aback. He trembled like a leaf. This gave me assurance, and I held him uneasy, causing the blood to run where I touched him with the ends of my fingers.[41]

The life and death struggle is, as Hegel points out, the relation of two independent self-consciousnesses, each believing itself to be absolute and each seeking the death of the other. In what Douglass says above, it has to be emphasized that, once he "resolves" to fight, it is not a dependent but an independent consciousness that is face-to-face with Covey. In this confrontation what terrifies Covey reinforces Douglass. This reversal, furthermore, is nothing more than the recognition by the formerly enslaved—Douglass—that in staking his life and in confrontation he has undermined the mastery of Covey—the concrete master—and forced him to shake and tremble, much like slaves grovel at the feet of their enslavers. In this, then, there is a reversal of roles between the master and the slave.[42] As Covey quakes— in equal measure—Douglass gains recognition both in his own eyes and in the eyes of his enslaver, who cannot anymore see him as a mere object of his persecution. Indeed, as Douglass tells us, "The whole six months afterwards, that I spent with Mr. Covey, he never laid the weight of his finger upon me. . . . This battle with Mr. Covey was the turning-point in my career as a slave. It rekindled the few expiring embers of freedom, and revived within me a sense of my own manhood."[43] This, then, is the conflictual process through which "a slave was made a man." As should be clear from all that has been said thus far, both Demby and Douglass are able to confront their enslavers only to the extent that they overcome the internalized fear and terror that keep them in their cowering and enslaved condition. As we noted with Hegel, this process of the lived self-overcoming through the negativity of experience is, thus, the concrete process through which recognition is attained.

Indeed, as we noted earlier with Fanon, "the American Negro . . . battles and is battled. . . . Nothing is . . . given free. . . . There is war, there are defeats, truces, [and] victories."[44] This dire struggle through which African American existence has made itself what it is was inaugurated in the—collective and singular—desperate combat of the enslaved who first challenged our subjugation and, over time, produced for us a heritage of "defeats, truces, [and] victories" that today constitute the truth of our existence.

But what is the truth of this heritage? It is the dialectical self-overcoming and self-unfolding of our existence in and out of the negativity of our lived experience. Demby, Douglass, and countless others asserted their freedom in overcoming the internalized conditions of their own enslavement. They reclaimed freedom out of the negativity of their existence. This is what Hegel refers to as the "inner self-movement of the content itself," that is, the dialectic.

As we saw in chapter 2, it is this concrete process of self-overcoming—understood as an uncompromising struggle against segregation—that Du Bois reclaims from within the concerns, and in the language, of his time. In like manner, we of the present, in looking at slave narratives and in our more recent past at Du Bois, have to recognize the lived dialectic of self-overcoming that is internal to our inheritance and actualize the possibility of further consolidating our inheritance of struggle.

Ferguson is right: in Hegel we do have a conceptualization of the dialectic of recognition that is of cardinal importance for grasping the truth of slave narratives.[45] This truth, however, is not the withdrawal of recognition but the consummation—and thus surpassing—of enslavement in the conflictual and dialectical recognition of autonomy and freedom. For, when all is said and done, in the poetic words of Maya Angelou, we are "the dream and the hope of the slave."[46]

4

Africa and Identity: Kwame Anthony Appiah and the Politics of Philosophy

An earlier version of this chapter titled "Comments on *In My Father's House*" was presented at the American Philosophical Association, Central Division, Ninety-third Annual Meeting in Chicago, April 1995. I read the paper as part of the session on Appiah's book *In My Father's House*.[1] The discussion that followed (Lawrence Blum's, Robert Gooding-Williams's, my paper, and Appiah's comments) was focused on questions of race and identity within the context of contemporary African American life and thought. Appiah's comments were also, to my hearing, focused on these same important and relevant questions. In the bargain, however, questions to do with African philosophy, politics, and questions of identity were not properly explored or engaged.

In view of the above it seemed proper to submit a second version of my presentation to *Research in African Literatures* in order to rouse and elicit a more energetic response to the concerns regarding Africa that Appiah's work has provoked.[2] For I strongly believe that an exchange on these and related issues should be of critical import to those of us concerned with the contemporary African situation. To my knowledge, however, this necessary discussion has not, thus far, taken place.

This chapter, then, is an attempt to provoke, for the third time and in a cordial way, a dialogue in the best Socratic sense of the word. For as Plato tells us, philosophy is focused on "the manner of one's life,"[3] and reflection, at its best, is aimed at comprehending "one's whole manner of living."[4] Appiah's views make questionable our contemporary African self-understanding of who we are — in the "manner" in which we comprehend our lived contemporary situation — thus they need to be critically interrogated.

I

As V. Y. Mudimbe has noted on the back jacket, Appiah's book is indeed "a major contribution to the field of African philosophy." It is a study grounded in a deep understanding of the issues it explores and presents with assuredness and a calm, confident tranquility. This is the kind of work that succinctly formulates and poses the relevant and enduring question of the field in which it operates. In agreement or in critical disagreement, it is a work that commands respect and appreciation.

To be sure, *In My Father's House* is not, as Appiah himself points out, a work that restricts itself or that could be restricted to "a single theme." The book is composed of four "clusters," the first three of which contain two chapters each and the last of which contains three chapters. The focus of my discussion is clusters three and four, whose main concerns are questions of philosophy, politics, and issues of identity as they pertain to the play and/or dialectic of the modern and the traditional in Africa.

While focusing on these two clusters, however, I will also make sporadic forays, as needed, in other directions. Indeed, *In My Father's House* has "many mansions," and it is to the dwelling of my own—and thus our shared—ancestors that I will turn my attention. For to systematically query and explore the resources and limitations of our shared heritage is a concern I wholeheartedly, if differently, share with Appiah. However, as the reader will see, I dwell in and speak from a realm in our shared ancestral abode that Appiah seldom visits.[5]

II

Today, in the closing years of the last decade of the twentieth century, fundamental questions of philosophy, politics, and identity are not only appropriate but necessary and should evoke thought if the African continent is to surmount the many difficulties that its *various* and *differing* peoples share. This is, as I have argued elsewhere, the fundamental task of contemporary African philosophy.[6]

The two clusters of Appiah's book on which this chapter is focused are engaged with questions that, in one way or another, show their relevance in the tragedies (Rwanda, Somalia) and triumphs (Ethiopia, Eritrea) that mark the contemporary political self-formation of the continent.[7] To critically reflect on this self-formation is itself to actively partake in, for better or for worse, this self-formative process. This critical engagement is, furthermore, an act of service in the realm of theory, focused on clarity and aimed at contributing toward Africa's own concrete and historical self-creation. It is an essential theoretic supplement to the tangible-practical efforts at emancipation—against Euro-American hegemony, neocolonialism—that are still unfolding against tremendous odds.[8]

African philosophy, as practiced on this side of the Atlantic, then, is not, in my view, rendered impotent by the distance from which it speaks. In fact, given the academic and political difficulties on the continent, distance allows one a favorable horizon within which critical questions can be properly explored. It establishes a material detachment that is fruitful in exploring that which is closest to our spiritual concerns. In this regard the politics of our theoretic interventions—even at such a distance—have effects that we cannot escape by claiming to be "pure" intellectuals engaged in the pursuit of "pure" truth.[9] In this regard naïveté has direct and dire political consequences, be they intended or unintended.

III

In the third cluster of his book, composed of two chapters—"Ethnophilosophy and Its Critics" and "Old Gods, New Worlds"—Appiah examines the question of the nature and status of African philosophy and the contemporary actuality of Africa in which old and new beliefs endure and are commingled under contemporary conditions. In this cluster, Appiah engages both the philosophic musings and the lived situation of contemporary Africa out of which these musings are emitted.

In "Ethnophilosophy and Its Critics," Appiah begins by noting that we, contemporary African philosophers, share, as part of our colonial legacy, in the analytic continental divide internal to the constitution of the European tradition of philosophy. To this extent, our philosophic practice must be aware and fully cognizant of the *impossibility* of "not bringing a Western philosophical training to bear" on our work.[10] In this acknowledgment of our lived colonial facticity and inheritance, what we need to do is be mindful of not injecting "Western ideas, along with . . . Western-derived methods, into the indigenous conceptual framework" as we engage in the exploration of traditional African systems of thought.[11]

In the above remarks Appiah has in mind the work of contemporary African ethnophilosophers. His point, however, is also one that can be validly made as a critique of Henry Odera Oruka's documentation of what he calls sage philosophy in Africa. This is so because Oruka fails to recognize that the interviews that produce the documents of sage philosophy are themselves products of a dialogue— partly inspired by the discourse of Western philosophy—and, thus, cannot produce, as he claims, a "pure" traditional African philosophy that is not affected or "contaminated" by the West.[12]

In contradistinction to the above, Appiah finds himself in partial agreement with Paulin Hountondji and Kwasi Wiredu. As he tells us, African philosophy is African for Hountondji and Wiredu not because it is "*about* African concepts or problems," as the ethnophilosophers think, but because "it is part of the universal discourse of philosophy that is carried on by Africans."[13] This is a restatement of Hountondji's geographic conception of African philosophy. In other words, African philosophy is "the universal discourse of philosophy" that is "carried on" by individuals who are the bearers of African passports. In and of itself, African philosophy has no themes and/or problems peculiar to itself.

Now, Marcien Towa, whom Appiah mistakenly lines up with Hountondji and Wiredu in the debate on African philosophy,[14] holds the view that "the current of thought represented by P. Hountondji [and Wiredu according to Appiah] does not occlude African thought, it openly excludes it."[15] This view, which Towa rejects categorically, is what I have just referred to in Appiah's approving restatement of it. In rejecting the ethnophilosophic assumption of the singular unanimity of traditional African thought, what needs doing, contra Hountondji's exclusion, is to explore the multiple variety of traditional African conceptions and views, not only "out of a concern for knowing ourselves" but also because "there is nothing that says we could not find anything precious in [these] conceptions."[16] Traditional African concepts and conceptions cannot and should not be dismissed a priori. For Towa—contra Appiah—African philosophy is about African "concepts" and "problems" and is, indeed, the "methodical and critical examination" of these concepts and problems in light of the concerns and exigencies of the present.[17]

To be sure, in the chapter with which we are concerned, Appiah, calling on the assistance of Kwame Gyekye, critically engages Ben Oguah's ethnophilosophic explorations in questions regarding Asanti Twi and Fanti Twi conceptions of the soul and of the human person.[18] In so doing, Appiah implicates himself in that which he denies. For he is exploring, with Oguah, African "concepts" and "problems" of the historical and cultural area that they share as Africans. Appiah, then, must be in agreement with Towa that the traditional cultures are worthy of exploration and examination. And yet he tells us, "Like Wiredu—and Hountondji—I aspire to a more truly critical discourse,"[19] that is, Hountondji's geographic conception.

But, then, how does Appiah account for Towa's rejection of the "current of thought" represented by Hountondji and Wiredu, considering that for these two thinkers, and especially for Hountondji, African philosophy is not "*about* African concepts or problems"?[20] For when Appiah says that he aspires "to a more truly critical discourse"—as evinced by his critical exchange with Oguah—he does have in mind a conception of African philosophy very similar to Towa's.[21] But does Towa not openly reject Hountondji's position, and is his political posture not at odds with Wiredu's restrained political stance? Appiah cannot have it both ways, for Towa stands in direct opposition to the perspective explicitly endorsed by him.

In "Old Gods, New Worlds," Appiah examines the pasticcio of spiritual beliefs in which contemporary Africa finds itself. Utilizing the example of a wedding between two modern and highly educated Africans, he recounts how traditional African religious beliefs and practices coexist along with the sacramental duties of a Methodist minister and a Catholic archbishop as part of the same ceremony. "These [the couple being wed], then, are modern Africans," Appiah tells us and names these and similar ceremonies "nontraditional."[22]

One is reminded of Sembène Ousmane's novel and film *Xala,* which is also centered on a wedding of modern Africans and exhibits a similar kind of pasticcio of traditional and modern in the sacrament of holy matrimony. For Sembène, this grotesque and uneven amalgam of intercultural forms is squarely situated in the domain of politics and in the context of Africa's subjection and neocolonial stasis. For Appiah, on the other hand, this is a serene and tranquil coexistence of differing faiths that is, according to him, accounted for by the African's belief in a variety of spiritual beings. As he puts it, "It is this belief in the plurality of invisible spiritual forces that makes possible the—to Western eyes—extraordinary spectacle of a Catholic bishop praying at a Methodist wedding in tandem with traditional royal appeal to the ancestors."[23] Appiah says the above after having noted that the "social organization of inquiry" in traditional Africa, in contradistinction to the approach of modern science,[24] as Robin Horton has observed, is "accommodative" as opposed to adversarial in style.[25] To this extent the scrutiny and critical assessment of differing theories are not possible; rather, diverse views are accommodated and can coexist. The "image of constant change"[26] and, to this extent, the critical bent of mind that goes with it, are absent in traditional African societies in which "accommodating conflicting theoretical views is part of the general process of accommodation necessary for those who are bound to each other as neighbors for life."[27] Add to this the lack of literacy—keeping in mind the African's penchant for "belief in the plurality of invisible spiritual forces"—and we have a situation in which old lore is statically echoed and passed on and critical thought is left by the wayside.[28]

To be sure, as Appiah notes, literacy is not a sufficient condition for the development of a scientific culture. Indeed, Appiah points to China,[29] but one could also point to ancient Abyssinia, a literate traditional culture whose literacy never left its clerical confines. It seems to me, however, that Appiah's whole presentation leaves out the grounding core, the political aspect, of this pasticcio which is the heart of the problem.

If today it is a fact that a "plurality of invisible spiritual forces" reign in Africa, this has more to do with the politico-cultural actualities of the continent than with the character of "the social organization of inquiry" in traditional Africa or with some strange African proclivity for believing in multiple spiritual forces.[30] For as one can see in Sembène's *Xala,* the "nontraditional" pasticcio that is contemporary Africa is a negative effect of the subordinate insertion of Africa into the modern world. As Sembène tells us, El Hadji Abdou Kader Beye, the central character of *Xala,* is the embodiment of an incomplete and unstable fusion of the business attitudes of the "European middle class" and of "a feudal African education" who makes "skilful use" of this volatile "dual background."[31] The xala or impotence that forces him to turn to the traditional culture for a magical cure is the effect of the collapse of this unstable union. It has nothing to do with a bent for believing in a "plurality" of spiritual forces.

In the person of El Hadji we see the xala, the paradoxical actuality of the counterfeit bourgeoisie, that Frantz Fanon examines in *Les Damnés de la terre.* And as Towa has convincingly argued in "Propositions sur l'identité culturelle" ("Propositions on Cultural Identity"),[32] this and similar problems can all be traced to the effects of the subjugated insertion of Africa into the modern world and the enduring negative effects of this insertion on the spiritual and cultural self-formation of modern Africans.

Indeed, the "Old Gods" of traditional Africa find themselves in "New Worlds,"

worlds that have as their singular divinity the commodification of every aspect of life. If in this duplicitous situation contemporary Africans engage in duplicity, this has nothing to do—contra Appiah—with an African proclivity or predisposition toward belief in multiple spiritual forces. It is, rather, the effect of a lived existential-political default: a compromise in which what is compromised is the potency of Westernized Africa and what is squandered is the possibility of reclaiming our existence as historical beings. The obverse of this compromise is Fanon's rejection of imitation or Amilcar Cabral's "return to the source."[33] Of course, none of this is of much use, significance, or interest to Appiah.

In "Altered States," Appiah discusses in some detail how the failures or administrative/political default of the state inherited from colonialism have created a situation in which traditional forms of organization (i.e., nonofficial Africa) concretely resurface and displace the functions of the state. Indeed this is, as Appiah puts it, "a universal phenomenon in postcolonial Africa."[34] It is the positive manifestation, in society, of the unstable fusion personified in El Hadji Abdou Kader Beye.

Indeed, the image that graces the cover of Appiah's book ("Man with a Bicycle") is a positive instance of this fusion. As Appiah himself notes,[35] this "polyglot" figure exemplifies the actuality of contemporary Africa and shows how, without a lot of pomp and fanfare, *nonofficial Africa* survives by concretely engaging the "dialectic of needs" in spite of its present neocolonial situation.[36] The "polyglot" figure is in fact a practical illustration of how the stasis of our postcolonial situation can be overcome. It is a specific and limited example of the kind of practical and engaged overcoming of a stagnant neocolonial situation that Chinua Achebe suggests at the end of *Anthills of the Savannah*.[37] Should we—those of us engaged in theoretic work—not think through the possibility of this polyglotism and query its beneficial implications?

As Appiah himself has noted, in "The Postcolonial and the Postmodern," the *post* in postcolonial is marked by thirty years of stagnation, suffering, and political impotence. It is this situation that creates on the one hand the suppression of traditional African cultures and on the other the coexistence, in subordination, of aspects of these same cultures with new cultural importations from the West. This is what Fanon refers to as the mummification of the colonized. And it is by a "return to the source,"[38] as Cabral formulates it, and not in terms of an "ethical universal,"[39] as Appiah suggests, that the emancipatory possibilities of this situation unfold. Indeed, this is what Sembène's *Xala* suggests in its cathartic conclusion. This, too, is what the Eritrean resistance shows in its thirty years of armed struggle.[40]

Unlike the West, for Africa, the experience of modernization was not the result of an internal process or dialectic of self-transformation but the result of conquest and subordination. The contradictory spirituality of contemporary Africans is, thus, itself a reflection of the paradoxical and distorted nature of modern Africa in the context of an imperialist and neocolonialist global politics of domination.[41]

As Sembène has suggested in *The Last of the Empire,* this pasticcio can be overcome only by forging "a synthesis [which is not] a step backwards [but a] new type of society" that properly blends our fractured present,[42] through which the pasticcio of "spiritual forces" reigns in our lives. This is also the task, on a conceptual level, that Towa suggests as the proper positive task for the contemporary discourse of African philosophy. Appiah, however, does little in this regard: Is philosophy, then, merely a negative critique?

IV

In "The Myth of an African World" and "African Identities," Appiah explores the tensions between our African identity and our specific ethnic identities. He questions the validity and actuality of a "metaphysical or mythic unity" or of a singular "African worldview."[43] Beyond these notions and conceptions, Appiah notes that "African unity" and "African identity . . . need securer foundations than race."[44] I, for one, do not find these considerations "disconcerting" in the least.[45] I wholeheartedly agree. And being an Eritrean I have concretely lived and experienced the negative effects of the essentialist perspective he is arguing against.

In my view, the theoretic legacies of the African liberation struggle as a whole can and should be properly explored and engaged, as regards its coherence, validity, and utility, in view of the contemporary situation of the continent. It is the critical appropriation of this heritage, in light of our contemporary political and historical needs, that has served and can still serve as the secure foundation of "African unity" and "African identity." For as Nkrumah, Lumumba, Cabral, Isayas, and many others have noted, the critical self-consciousness of this heritage has always been articulated in terms of Africa. It was never a question or a concern with ethnic and/or "race" politics as such.

Indeed, beyond our ethnic identities, the heritage of the differing African liberation movements makes possible for us a historical and political world in which we all share as Africans. This "sharing" does not presuppose any kind of racial, mystical, or metaphysical African oneness. It only calls for the recognition that, beyond color and race, our being African is grounded in a shared history of subjugation, struggle, and political liberation: a history we affirm, choose to perpetuate, and aim to further expand on and consolidate! And even when we choose against it, we do so from within its context and lived ambient. For to be a modern African is necessarily to have been affected not only by the colonial experience but also by that which brought this experience to an end. And this, furthermore, is not a question of choice.

It is in this sense that Cabral talks about the struggle for African liberation as a "return to the source." In like manner, Fanon, in *The Wretched of the Earth* and earlier in *Black Skin, White Masks,* points to the historical limitations of Négritude and of the idea of a sub-Saharan continental African/Negro culture. Indeed, the present African continental and national identities are constructions negotiated in adverse situations and under hostile and violent political conditions. This does not make them any less real or actual![46] It should be noted that the weight of history is not always negative. In the thirty or so years in which most of Africa has been nominally independent, these constructed and "artificial" nation-states have not shown a persistent propensity for disintegration. On the contrary, as the thirty-year Eritrean resistance against Ethiopian occupation has shown, it seems that the artificial borders established by imperial Europe have formed into concrete and lived historical identities.[47]

In view of all of the above, I strongly disagree with Appiah when he says that to be African is "a usable identity,"[48] that "African identity is, for its bearers, only one among many,"[49] or that "there are times when Africa is not the banner we need."[50] To recognize that we are all historical beings and the bearers of multiple identities—the traces of our lived historicity—or that we need to discard metaphysical, mystical, or essentialist notions about Africa is not in any way equal to affirming that Africa is a "usable identity." Furthermore, the constructed nature of our identities is not something peculiar to Africans.

Indeed, as Appiah himself recognizes, one could affirm the same of Europe, America, or Asia.[51] And yet the tone and character of Appiah's whole discussion overstate his legitimate critique of essentialism and put into question the very idea of the historical actuality of a concrete African identity as such. In fact, Appiah is aware of this, for he feels the need to reassure his readers that we indeed are "Africans already" and that the reality of our being African is embodied in "numerous examples from multiple domains."[52] This obsessive need to reassure us betrays Appiah's unease precisely because his case is overstated and threatens any historically grounded notion of African identity per se. As an old Tigringia proverb has it, "Serák mebái beálu yiléfálef," which literally translated states, "He who steals from the charity box exposes himself."

It is not that Africa is our collective "charity box"; rather, it is the name we give to our collective if variegated *story*. And "the story," as Achebe has noted, is that which

> continue[s] beyond the war and the warrior. It is the story that outlives the sound of war-drums and the exploits of brave fighters. It is the story . . . that saves our progeny from blundering like blind beggars into the spikes of the cactus fence. The story is our escort; without it, we are blind. Does the blind man own his escort? No, neither do we the story; rather *it is the story that owns us and directs us*. It is the thing that makes us different from cattle.[53]

Appiah's critique of essentialism oversteps its bounds and puts into question the very actuality of "the story," that is, of a concretely constituted and historically grounded African identity. Appiah forgets that he too—as he writes—is owned by "the story" and that the theoretic positions he articulates are choreographed and "directed" by the very identity he puts into question: a concretely lived and varie-gated identity. Appiah forgets the very "thing that makes us different from cattle"! The lived actuality of this identity, furthermore, is attested to not only by nov-elists and their fictional characters but by those engaged in the actual process of African self-formation. Speaking to the Organization of African Unity (OAU)—after thirty years of struggle and as many years of OAU malignant neglect—the president of newly independent Eritrea, Isayas Afwerki, stated, among other things, "In this regard, I must admit that we have sought membership in the orga-nization [i.e., the OAU] not because we have been impressed by its achievements but, as a local proverb goes, in the spirit of familial obligation; because we are keenly aware that what is ours is ours."[54] Indeed, what is "ours is ours"! Our African identity is not something "usable," for we never use it and then "put it away." Rather, it is the concrete actuality of our existence as beings that are human. It is the "story that owns us and directs us" and within which we live and own up to the actuality of our existence. Indeed, as Hans-Georg Gadamer has noted, in an analogous context, "In fact history [i.e., the story] does not belong to us, but we belong to it. Long before we understand ourselves through the process of self-examination, we understand ourselves in a self-evident way in the family, society and state in which we live."[55] This is what Afwerki means when he states that, in spite of everything, "we are keenly aware that what is ours is ours," for "in the final analysis" the Eritrean achievement "is and remains an African achieve-ment."[56]

To affirm the reverse of the above, under whatever pretext (i.e., in an effort to pay back the OAU in kind!), would have been a futile mimicry, in reverse, on Af-werki's part, of the OAU's callous inattentiveness to our collective *story* as Africans. It would also have been an endorsement of Appiah's ephemeral idea that to be an African is a "usable identity." But, after Freud, after Nietzsche, after Hei-degger, can such claims—that finite beings have a clear and transparent view of their "usable" identities—be taken seriously?

V

As Marx noted long ago, human beings make their own history but not under con-ditions of their own choosing. Our identities (i.e., our stories) are historical-political constructs. But this does *not* make the "effective-history" that constitutes our being something we use and put away. We live, as human beings, in and as the story/identity that we are.

In this regard, it should be noted that Placide Tempels's *Bantu Philosophy*, which inaugurates the contemporary discourse of African philosophy, was politi-cally aimed at undermining the traditional ethnic identities of indigenous Africans in the service of colonialism. As is well known, Tempels's aim in writing this book was to assist the European "civilizing mission" by exposing and appropriating the intellectual productions of the Bantu/African in order to better anchor the colonialist project in the consciousness of the colonized.

As Ernest Wamba-dia-Wamba has suggested, the practice of African philosophy ought to be aimed at reversing Tempels's efforts in the service of the concrete self-emancipation of the peoples of Africa.[57] In like manner, as Theophilus Okere has noted, the discourse of contemporary African philosophy is itself an intellectual product of the process of further articulating the actuality of our African identity in the context of our present postcolonial situation.[58] To claim an identity is to interpretatively appropriate a heritage. For identities are historical-political actualities and, thus, are fluid and always in an ongoing process of interpretation and reinterpretation.

When Aimé Césaire—in contradistinction to Léopold Sedar Senghor—affirms that Négritude is a "concrete rather than an abstract coming to consciousness,"[59] and an affirmation of our blackness, or when Patrice Lumumba writes that "we are Africans and wish to remain so,"[60] what is being upheld is not a "metaphysical or mythic unity" but a concrete identity in the context of social, political, and historic struggles. What is being affirmed is the actuality of our collective *story,* that is, of that which, as Achebe puts it, "makes us different from cattle." The importance of this cannot be overemphasized, for, until quite recently, the civilized—that is, the European—world did not consider us much different than cattle.[61]

As Cabral noted in 1962, the United Nations "resolution on decolonization" affirms and is in turn affirmed by the African struggle to reclaim our story/identity as human beings.[62] Thus, the legacy of postcolonial humanity harbors within it the positive achievements of the African anticolonial struggle, a struggle for our African identity. This, then, is what we too need to appropriate and further expand on in the context of the concrete problems and issues of the last decade of the twentieth century. For our identities are not "usable"—but neither are they static. In being the concretizations of a lived heritage, their constancy is constituted by the fluidity of always being open to the hoped-for and the possible.[63] To this extent, then, to be an African is not a "usable identity" but the actuality of a specific and lived heritage.

In the words of the founding poet of Négritude, what we need to do, on the level of theory, is to properly engage the

singularité de notre "situation dans le monde" qui ne se confond avec nulle autre. Singularité de nos problémes qui ne se raménent á nul autre problème. Singularité de notre histoire coupée de terribles avatars qui n'appartiennent qu'á elle. Singularité de notre culture que nous voulons vivre de manière de plus en plus réelle. [singularity of our "situation in the world," which is not to be confused with any other situation. The singularity of our problem, which is not subsidiary to any other problem. The singularity of our history, laced with terrible misfortunes which belong to no other history. The singularity of our culture, which we intend to live and actualize in a much more concrete manner.][64]

We are all inheritors of a past that is not open to our manipulation or control and which constitutes our lived present and the possibilities of our future.[65] The project of African philosophy, viewed in this light, then, is aimed at exploring the possibilities and deficiencies of this history. It is all of this that Appiah puts into question with his ephemeral idea of a "usable identity."

VI

I would like to conclude by saying that, to critique, in the best sense of the term, is not to say "bad things" of and/or "attack" a text; rather, it is to open up a text or an issue to questioning and further exploration. It is to engage in a concrete questioning along with the text and, in the example of Socrates and Zär'a Ya'aqob, to search out the limitations, ramifications, and possibilities located in the conceptions and ideas of a text.

In this sense, then, a critique is a *hatäta,* a questioning, "the methodical and critical examination" that constitutes the practice of philosophy. This is what I hope my reflections contribute to the discussion of Appiah's book.

5

African Philosophy? Looking behind the Question

As Benjamin E. Oguah has noted, until very recently the very idea of African philosophy was enough "to cause scornful or, at least, skeptical laughter in certain quarters in the west."[1] As of late, however, this narrow-minded and Eurocentric hilarity has begun to subside. Major publishers such as Routledge, Blackwell, Rowman and Littlefield, Oxford, and so on, have taken it upon themselves to publish monographs and anthologies in this area of research and study.[2]

Contemporary philosophy textbooks, furthermore, no longer limit themselves to an exposition of European thought with an Oriental supplement at the end for good measure.[3] Robert C. Solomon's *A Short History of Philosophy,* under the general heading "From Modernism to Postmodernism: The Twentieth Century," has an interesting section entitled "The Return of the Oppressed: Africa, Asia, and the Americas."[4] In like manner, David E. Cooper's *World Philosophies,* under the general heading "Recent Non-Western Philosophies," has an engaging discussion of African philosophy.[5]

To be sure, the pages dedicated to African and non-European philosophies in these texts are rather slender. But meager as these sections are, they challenge, at a fundamental level, the Eurocentric idea that philosophy is singularly indigenous only to the West. In other words, Martin Heidegger's view that "the statement that philosophy is in its nature Greek says nothing more than that the West and Europe, and only these, are, in the innermost course of their history, originally 'philosophical.'"[6] On Cornelius Castoriadis's more recent assertion that "among the creations in our history, Greco-Western history, there is one that we judge positively and take credit for: putting things into question, criticizing them, requiring a *logon didonai*—accounting for something and giving a reason for it—which is the presupposition for both philosophy and politics."[7] More and more such views are beginning to be seen as nothing more than "a gratuitous prejudice."[8] And so, when we look behind the puzzled and/or incredulous question that some of us used to and still do face—"African philosophy?!"—what we find is a studied bigotry and/or a myopic view of the West and the rest of us.

Needless to say, this Eurocentric bias/perspective that is quick to "credit" the "Greco-Western" tradition or "the West and Europe, and only these," with all the positive accretions of human historical becoming could itself benefit from a mild dose of the same kind of questioning it is so jealously possessive of. Chapter 6 will present such a questioning of the central icons of the modern tradition of European philosophy. Presently, however, I would like to begin by taking this "gratuitous prejudice" at face value and seeing if indeed there is such a thing as traditional African philosophy or philosophical thinking.[9] I will then turn to the need to reorient African philosophic work toward indigenous sources and to do so out of the exigencies of the present. And, in this context, I will engage questions of dependence and/or "development" in that which Marcien Towa alludes to as "notre identité humaine générique" [our generic human identity].

I

As Claude Sumner points out in introducing the volume composed of the twenty-five papers presented at the First Pan-African Symposium on the "Problematics of an African Philosophy" in 1976, the basic topic "of discussion [was] the existence and nature of African Philosophy."[10] Sumner's own contribution to the symposium and to the ongoing discussion in and on African philosophy,[11] among other things, has been to make the work of Zär'a Ya'aqob and his student Wälda Hey-wát—both seventeenth-century Abyssinian philosophers—available in translation for contemporary use.[12]

But who are these thinkers? And are they, indeed, philosophers? In order to respond to these questions in a fruitful manner, we need to utilize "a classical procedure: indicate that which philosophy is in general, or at least that which one means by it *[entend par-là]*, and then demonstrate consequently how different philosophies are articulated interior to this notion of philosophy."[13] In responding to the above, we thus need to make a detour by way of René Descartes and Immanuel Kant: philosophers whose philosophical credentials are indubitable!

Keeping the above "classical procedure" in mind, if we take a quick glance at the discourse of modern European philosophy that begins with Descartes, we note that it has its origins in the concerns arising from the gradual disintegration of the medieval tradition and the opening up of the horizon of modern science. As Romano Guardini tells us, "The Medieval picture of the world along with the cultural [philosophic] order which it supported began to dissolve during the fourteenth century. The process of dissolution continued throughout the fifteenth and sixteenth centuries. By the seventeenth century it was complete, and a new picture of reality dawned clearly and distinctly over Europe."[14] An integral and central component of this "new picture of reality" was the emergence of a "new notion of science and method" that was "worked out initially in a partial field of study by Galileo and philosophically grounded for the first time by Descartes."[15] Descartes's methodic doubt grounded this new notion of science and method on the abstract intellectual subjectivity of the disembodied ego. In so doing he limited valid knowledge to the *res extensa* that could be grasped and expressed in mathematical terms, thus curtailing the realm of knowledge and establishing the basic presupposition necessary for the development of scientism.

The further amplification of this "new picture of reality," which, by the seventeenth century, had "clearly and distinctly" emerged "over Europe," also made possible Kant's Copernican Revolution, which enshrined the subjectivity of the subject as the originative moment of reflection for modern European thought. Kant continued on Descartes's course by establishing the a priori conditions of the possibility for scientific knowledge. Limiting valid knowledge to the realm of the phenomenal, and thus denying knowledge, he made room for faith.[16]

The "divorce . . . between *fides* [faith] and *ratio* [reason],"[17] the demise of medieval philosophy, necessitated a new and indubitable grounding of ratio. By articulating this grounding, Descartes and Kant became cornerstones of modern European thought. Both labored in the process of fabricating this new *horizon,* and synchronously, in a dialectical manner, their labor of thought—in the character of its concerns—was called into being by the theoretic exigencies of their time. But how exactly did they do this? They did it by being open to, and critically inventorying,[18] their heritage in terms of the theoretic demands of the "new picture of reality" that had "clearly and distinctly" emerged on the horizon of the Europe of their day.[19]

In view of the above, if we look at Descartes in contrast to the medieval tradition from which he was trying to distance himself or at Kant in the *Critique of Pure Reason* when he tells us that we "must approach nature in order to be taught by it. . . . not however . . . in the character of a pupil who listens to everything that the teacher chooses to say, but of an appointed judge who compels the witnesses to answer questions which he has himself formulated,"[20] we see that both of these European thinkers are engaged in a "methodical and critical examination" of concerns that are ultimately derived from the crisis provoked by the "divorce" of faith from reason.[21] It is within the horizon of this paradigm shift that both Descartes and Kant make their mark.

In keeping with our detour—the "classical procedure" indicated above—we can, thus, say that philosophy is an *open, critical,* and *methodic* inventory of the grounding questions of a specific horizon and/or moment of time. Or, as Marcien Towa puts it, philosophy

> presents itself as an ensemble of works labeled *[dits]* philosophical. The reading of such works imposes, it seems to us, the idea that philosophy is the courage to think the absolute. The human being thinks, and of all *known* beings, he is the only one that thinks. Thought is taken here in a restrictive sense: in the sense of weighing, discussing representations, beliefs, opinions, confronting them, examining the pros and cons of each, *selecting critically,* in order to retain only the ones that stand-up to the test of criticism and classification. In this restrictive sense, representations, convictions, opinions that have not endured *[subi]* the test of criticism or have not survived it, are not thoughts or ideas, but simple beliefs.[22]

What we need to do next is ask the critical question: Given this conception, do the Abyssinian thinkers pass muster? The thinking of Zär'a Ya'aqob (and his student Wälda Heywát)[23] is located in the radically different—from Europe—terrain of seventeenth-century Abyssinia. Unlike their European counterparts, they are not concerned with—and have no reason to be concerned with!—the "divorce" of faith and reason and the ensuing crisis of European rationality. Their concern is with the question of piety in the context of the acute crisis of Abyssinian Coptic Christianity in confronting the subversive work of Catholic missionaries. Provoked by this particular confrontation—of two differing renditions of Christianity—the *hatäta* of Zär'a Ya'aqob is involved with religiosity *as such* in its differing and, thus, bewildering claims and manifestations.

In this Ya'aqob is not concerned with defending the faith of his forefathers. He is not engaged in presenting a defensive tract, an apologetic documentation of his tradition, even though it is this tradition that internally structures the very substance of his thinking. Indeed, as he tells us,

> Man aspires to know truth and the hidden things of nature, but this endeavour is difficult and can only be attained with great labour and patience, as Solomon (Ecclesiastes 1:13) said: "With the help of wisdom I have been at pains to study all that is done under heaven; oh, what a weary task God has given mankind to labour at!" Hence people hastily accept what they have heard from their fathers and shy from any (critical) examination. But God created man to be the master of his own actions, so that he will be what he wills to be, good or bad.[24]

Nor is Zär'a Ya'aqob concerned only with the particular and singular issue that occasioned his thinking. Deeply steeped in the classical learning of Abyssinian Coptic Christianity, he is concerned with presenting a hatäta, a critical "inventory" of faith as manifested in differing practices of piety.[25] The ethical possibility for man to be "master of his own actions" such that "he will be what he wills to be" is the core concern of his thinking. Thus, the freedom of man, in the grace of God, is the central preoccupation that moves Zär'a Ya'aqob's thought.

From within the ambient of the concerns of his own heritage, the horizon of his time/culture, Zär'a Ya'aqob's hatäta parallels the thinking of Descartes and Kant. In substantive terms, on the other hand, it is akin to Socrates's query in the *Euthyphro*. But at this point, one might ask, What exactly does the word *hatäta* mean? As Sumner reminds us, this Ge'ez word literally means "to question bit by bit, piece-meal; to search into or through, to investigate accurately; to examine; to inspect."[26] In other words, it is to engage in an open, critical, and methodic inventory of a question and/or issue from within the ambient of a specific horizon. This methodical and systematic exploration of a question in seeking its "whatness" was, for the ancient Greeks, the proper task of philosophy.

This is what Castoriadis refers to as "putting things into question, criticizing them, requiring a logon didonai . . . which is the presupposition for . . . philoso-phy."[27] But is this not just what Zär'a Ya'aqob is doing in his hatäta? In ques-tioning—in matters of faith—that which "people hastily accept . . . from their fathers,"[28] is he not seeking for and "requiring a logon didonai"? Indeed, he is.

Long before Kant, Zär'a Ya'aqob sits in judgment and acts as "an appointed judge who [probes and] compels the witnesses to answer questions which he has himself formulated."[29] He engages the readers, whom he addresses directly (à la Descartes) and invites them to reflect on the dubious veracity of differing tradi-tions of faith as manifested in Islam, Judaism, and Christianity—in both its Cop-tic and Catholic versions. The difference that one sees in Descartes and Kant on the one hand and Zär'a Ya'aqob on the other is not in the "specific type of intel-lectual activity"[30] that each engages in but, rather, in the cultural, historical, intel-lectual content—the horizon—within which each articulates this "type of intel-lectual activity." What we have to keep in mind, in each case, is that

> philosophers . . . are not themselves abstractions, but . . . beings of flesh and bones who belong to a continent, to a particular culture, and to a specific period. And for a particular philosopher, to really philosophize is necessarily to examine in a critical and methodic manner the essential problems of his milieu and of his period. He will thus elaborate a philosophy that is in an explicit or implicit relation with his times and his milieu.[31]

In other words, "every individual is a child of his time; so philosophy too is its own time apprehended in thoughts."[32] It is the open, critical, and methodic inventory—a thoughtful pondering—of the central and lived concerns of a horizon and/or moment of time.

In concluding our detour—the "classical procedure" with which we began—we can conclusively say that Zär'a Ya'aqob's thinking is a concrete example of tra-ditional African philosophy, an autochthonous philosophical thinking that does not owe anything to the European tradition of thought. Thus, and in this regard, Heidegger and Castoriadis—on their own terms—express nothing more than a "gratuitous prejudice" when they claim that philosophic thought is singularly indigenous only to the West—and not only in this regard!

Towa has decisively shown, in a detailed examination of "les contes des cycles sapientiaux,"[33] of the "oral literature that can still be gathered today among Africans living in a traditional milieu,"[34] that "the principal preoccupation" in this literature is "the teaching of stratagems, prudence and reflection."[35] In these tales, "il s'agit de mettre l'adversaire dans une situation qui l'aménera à reconnaître et à proclamer par intérêt ce qu'il refusait d'admettre par intérêt" [it is a question of putting the adversary in a situation such that he will own up to that which he opposed out of partiality].[36] But why is such a ruse necessary? It is necessary because "celui dont les opinions sont dictées par les passions est insensible à l'ar-gumentation purement abstraite. Pour changer ses opinion il faut et il suffit de changer la direction de ses désirs" [he whose views are dictated by passion is not open to abstract argumentation. To change his views it is necessary to change the direction of his passions].[37] But is this stratagem not the same as Socratic irony? Listen to what Guardini tells us, regarding Socratic irony, basing his ideas on a classic text in which this stratagem is put to deadly use:

> The *Euthyphro* is, among the texts with which we are concerned, that in which the irony of Socrates appears most clearly. . . . What does a man do when he treats another with irony? He makes him ridiculous. . . . [T]he wielder of irony . . . makes appreciative remarks, but in such a way that an unfavourable meaning appears through them. His assent only underlines the contradiction more plainly. He assumes an inoffensive air, only to wound the more surely. . . . All of this could be said of irony in general; but Socratic irony is more than this. In the last resort its object is not to expose, to wound, to despatch, but to help. It has a positive aim: to stimulate movement and to liberate. It aims at serving truth.[38]

Indeed, this, too, is the explicit purpose of the oral African "traditional thought" which is "essentially the exhaltation of intelligence in the service of justice,"[39] that is, in the service of "truth," within the limits of our lived finitude.

To be sure, and for good reason, this oral tradition is not concerned with "l'argumentation purement abstraite" [a purely abstract argument]. But then, are the dialogues of Plato (Socratic irony!), the aphorisms of Nietzsche, the dialectic of Hegel, or the meditations of the later Heidegger concerned with a purely abstract argumentation? From all that has been said above, then, we can categorically affirm that the question of African philosophy is "less a borrowing [or imitation] from European culture than a retrieval, a rejuvenation and re-valorizing of an *ancient heritage,* and, more profoundly, a re-conquest and re-affirmation of our *generic human identity.*"[40] The bewildered and incredulous hilarity that one encounters behind the question "African philosophy?!" is, then, at best nothing more than a myopic view and at worst a studied bigotry, a residue of bygone days, the "golden age" of the Enlightenment, when Europe confidently saw itself as the measure of humanity and/or civilization.[41]

Still, beyond this Eurocentric myopia, the question of African philosophy is directly bound up with the effort to retrieve "an ancient heritage" and in so doing reclaim "our generic human identity." What is required next is to explore the necessary bond between this retrieval—the reorienting of philosophic work toward indigenous sources—and our inherent African humanity.

II

We are, at the close of the twentieth century, at a point in time when the dominance of the *uni*verse of European singularity is being encompassed or engulfed by the *multi*verse of our shared humanity. The colonizer, self-deified imperial Europe, is dead! In this context, the central concern for the practice of philosophy focused on the formerly colonized world should be directed at helping to create a situation in which the enduring residue of our colonial past is systematically overcome.

This residue—the imperious/imperial self-image of colonial Europe—conserved and practiced by postcolonial elites is, for the most part, the defining characteristic of the African elites that have inherited postcolonial power. As Friedrich Nietzsche has noted, "God is dead; but given the way of men, there may still be caves for thousands of years in which his shadow will be shown.—And we—we still have to vanquish his shadow, too."[42] In vanquishing this shadow, or in order to vanquish the enduring shadow of the dead colonial God, it is necessary to put into question, systematically, the theoretic underpinnings of all that was "built upon this faith, propped up by it, grown into it."[43]

In the last decade of the twentieth century we are, on a formal level, beyond the constricting confines of colonialism. And yet every aspect of existence in the formerly colonized world, and in Africa specifically, is still, in essential and fundamental ways, determined and controlled by our former colonizers. I say this not in order to shift blame but to locate specifically the source of our present predicament, not only as it pertains to our economic and political dependence on the West, but also as it pertains to our dependence and subordinate position in the realm of thinking and questions of knowledge.

As Paulin J. Hountondji has noted, "Historically, science and technology, *in their present form* on the African continent, can be traced back to the colonial period."[44] Africa is still the site *from* which data and raw materials are collected and on which theoretical findings are applied. The decisive aspect of scientific and/or theoretic work, "the interpretation of raw information,"[45] or the formulation of the paradigmatic framework of scientific work and thinking always takes place beyond our shores. This deplorable situation, furthermore, is taken "for granted" and as "normal" by those engaged in such work.[46]

This interiorized hegemony of the West—our enduring "faith" in the "shadow" of the dead colonial God—finds its "objective"[47] correlate in "the historical integration and subordination of [our systems of knowledge] to the world system of knowledge and 'know-how,' just as underdevelopment as a whole results, primarily, not from any original backwardness, but from the integration of our subsistence economies into the world capitalist market."[48] On the subjective side, this equation—the concrete-material subordination of our societies that subtends our being a superfluous appendage of a "world system of knowledge"—is sustained and perpetuated, into the future, by an "ideology . . . of universalism,"[49] the matrix of the lived subjectivity and thinking of Westernized Africa. But what exactly does this mean, and how does it function?

As Immanuel Wallerstein has shown, "Universalism is a faith, as well as an epistemology";[50] it is "a set of beliefs about what is knowable and how it can be known."[51] This creed is the view that the natural-physical and social-historical worlds are accessible to a value-free neutral science and/or technic that achieves its results best when all "historically constrained elements" are removed from it.[52] This "concept of a neutral 'universal' [scientific] culture"[53] that makes accessible the truth of the social and natural world is "grafted onto 'national' variations"[54] under the guise of the spread of science, skills, knowledge, and general enlightenment and through a worldwide web of educational and cultural-political institutions.

Thus are created "cadres"[55] or "elites of peripheral areas"[56] that are, basically, the Trojan Horse of Euro-American global dominance. Surreptitiously mantled—especially to themselves—by this "universalism," it is in effect the hegemony of the West (i.e., the "historically constrained elements" that constitute its efficacious historical actuality) that is perpetuated, sustained, and conserved over time in and through these "cadres." This "universalism," in other words, is not imposed from the outside. It is lived and concretely actualized in and through us: Westernized Africa.[57] As Frantz Fanon noted not so long ago, in the Antilles—but also in Africa—when a student comes home, many times "it is a European who has arrived."[58]

The educated few—precisely because of their education in which so much hope is invested—regard the continent as a curse and remain faithful to their educational-cultural formation. Africa must transcend the vicious circularity of this *Gestell* (enframing)—the mold of Western dominance—if it is to effectively reclaim and carve out the space of its own freedom.[59] Given the actuality of this enframing, it would indeed be surprising if those Africans, trained and engaged in scientific and technical work, did not take *"for granted"* and as *"normal"* our subordinate position. For the abnormality of our dependence (addiction?) can be disclosed and/or glimpsed only by "destroy[ing]" or at least putting into question "the *myths* [universalism being the first of these myths] which, more than money or weapons, constitute the most formidable obstacle" to the regeneration of the formerly colonized world.[60] For the West, today, rules us not "through the force of its weapons" but in a much more intangible, pernicious, and efficacious manner. It rules us through us, our own lived concrete subjectivity, "through its ideas, through its 'models' of growth and development, through the statist and other structures which, having been created by it," have been internalized by us and "are today adopted everywhere."[61]

Thus, this "ideology of universalism" is not and does not function as merely a Euro-American or Western cultural egoism that insists on seeing and placing itself at and as the center of the world. More than this it is "a pervasive condition of thought" that "affects both Europeans and non-Europeans, despite the specific questions and situations that each may address."[62] Indeed, it is by way of these very "specific questions and situations" and as their sole "rational" and/or "scientific" solution that this ideology concretely manifests itself.

The fact that this is the character of our postcolonial situation should, in my view, be the point of entry for the concrete *reorientation of philosophic work toward indigenous sources*. Hountondji does well in pointing to our lamentable theoretic dependence on the West.[63] It is, however, necessary to go further and formulate the substantial thematic context in terms of which the source of this dependence can be critically explored and unhinged.

In this respect, African philosophic practice has to engage in the systematic and critical exploration of indigenous forms of knowledge: practical and theoretic. This focused and critical *Wiederholung* (repetition),[64] in Heidegger's formulation, or "return to the source,"[65] in Amilcar Cabral's terms,[66] aimed at sifting through and systematically appropriating—in terms of contemporary needs—aspects of our precolonial heritage of indigenous knowledge is the theoretic orientation that is needed in order to break the enframing mold of Western dominance in the realm of intellectual work and the production of knowledge. For "the more one realizes that the chief goal of the liberation movement goes beyond the achievement of political independence . . . the more evident is the necessity of undertaking a *selective analysis* of the values of the culture within the framework of the struggle for liberation."[67] It is this "selective analysis," within the contemporary context of our postcolonial situation, that we can and must make our own in the indigenous reorientation of philosophic work. For the aim of this "selective analysis"—for Cabral and for us—is the "*confluence* of . . . culture,"[68] traditional and modern, aimed at confronting the lived exigencies of the present. In this exigent reenacting of Cabral's "return to the source," our philosophic work would reorient itself toward indigenous sources[69] and in so doing, in effect put the enframing dominance of the West in question.

For it is not at going back to a past that cannot be but, rather, at going back to the lived possibilities of African existence closed off by colonial conquest and stifled, to this day, by neocolonial inertia that this "return to the source" is directed. It is in this way that the "struggle for philosophy" in Africa is directly tied to the struggle against the residue of "colonial racism" and the "ideological snares of neocolonialism."[70] The "showing" or "proving" that our African traditions have, or have had in the past, philosophy and philosophers is not in this regard the point at issue.[71] What is at issue is a much more concrete and practical matter.

We must prospect—holding our educated Eurocentric biases in abeyance—the know-how, skills, and wisdom of our heritages in view of critically updating them for contemporary use. And how is this to be done? It must be done by sifting through our legacies: retaining that which is alive, casting off that which is lethargic, and critically fusing the heritages of the past with modern scientific conceptions.[72] If viewed in this way, as a conscious, critical, and conscientious policy implemented in the differing and various realms—that is, politics, economics, education, cultural policy, urban planning, and so on—of contemporary African existence, the "return to the source" is the one way of breaking the vicious circularity of the mold within which Euro-America holds us captive.

In this theoretic framework, Zär'a Ya'aqob's hatäta is for us a paradigmatic example of the practice of African philosophy (hermeneutics?) that has been spun out of the horizon of seventeenth-century Abyssinia. The sapiential tales that

Towa examines so insightfully, in like manner, allow us to understand the use and role of reason in the life-world of traditional Africa. In all of this what we must do is "utilize the past with the intention of opening up the future,"[73] what Nietzsche refers to as the critical use of history in the service of life.[74]

What we have in mind, then, is a way of interpretatively exploring the possibilities of African existence within the ambient—needs and tools—of the present and out of the resources of our heritages. To be sure, "supernaturalism is a subjectivism which pretends to submit nature directly to arbitrary whims and desires, while technology [science] founds its actions on knowledge of and respect for determinism, that is to say on the objective regularity of natural processes."[75] But can all aspects of our African heritages be subsumed under the category of "supernaturalism"? The task of philosophy, here as elsewhere, is to proceed in a methodic and critical probing of these heritages aimed at discarding the sterile/lethargic and preserving/cultivating that which is vital precisely because it can be utilized for ameliorating and/or overcoming our deplorable situation. Utility, in this regard, is gauged in terms of the contemporary exigencies that the situation calls for and is fueled by and encompassed within the emancipatory foresight of the age-old African struggle for freedom.[76]

What, then, is this *situation,* and what does it call for? In order to properly address this last point, we need to engage the question of dependence and/or "development" in that which Towa alludes to as "notre identité humaine générique" [our generic human identity].

III

"The greatest actual difference between the Occident and Africa . . . is the difference between he who exercises the power of initiative and creativity and he who is deprived of it:"[77] In plain terms, this "difference"—which constitutes the core essence of our contemporary situation—was created *manu militari.* Starting in the fifteenth century and reaching its zenith by the end of the nineteenth century, imperial Europe enslaved the peoples of Africa and then colonized the continent as a whole minus the Kingdom of Abyssinia. In Marx's classic words,

> The discovery of gold and silver in America, the extirpation, enslavement and entombment in mines of the aboriginal population, the beginning of the conquest and looting of the East Indies, the turning of Africa into a warren for the commercial hunting of black-skins, signalised the rosy dawn of the era of capitalist production. These idyllic proceedings are the chief momenta of primitive accumulation.[78]

The enslavement of Africa, and its subsequent colonial parceling among the imperious nations of Europe as colonial domains, was a period of time when Africa was effectively blotted out of world history.[79] During this same period, modernity established itself. Synchronously, the problem of "underdevelopment" was created by the forced insertion of Africa's destroyed "subsistence economies into the world capitalist market."[80]

The originary moment of this insertion, furthermore, was made possible by the systematic destruction not only of the economies but—much more damning—of the whole fabric of life of the subjugated societies of Africa. As Towa puts it,

> The invaders, especially the missionaries, indulged in sheer cultural vandalism, destroying or looting works of art, and making war on our religions and beliefs [philosophies?]. Our leaders and political institutions became mere cogs in the colonial administrative machinery; our languages—storehouses of our cultural heritage—were forbidden; economic life was disrupted, skilled artisan crafts asphyxiated, etc. More damaging than this destruction of our cultures, was the loss of the *historic initiative*.[81]

In other words, Africans' mode of life, their human habitat, was unhinged and displaced—placed out of history—by conquest. Things African were devalued, and the African was first reduced to slavery and then subjugated to the passivity of being a colonial subject. This "subjectification,"[82] in its historical unfolding and actualization, has been the process whereby the peoples of Africa were "fitted, as a mere instrument, into a practical process,"[83] the practical-historical process of the establishment of European modernity, that is, global capitalism.

Locally, in "Western Europe,"[84] the originative site of its self-institution, the capitalist mode of production required proletarians—laborers doubly free from servile bondage and property. Globally, it required noncapitalistic (i.e., non-European) modes of life to be reduced to dependency. And this state of affairs is managed and maintained to this day in "independent" Africa by the neocolonial "cadres" or the "elites of peripheral areas" enlightened and formed by the epistemology and faith of "universalism." This, then, *grosso modo,* is the situation of contemporary Africa. What does it call for?

In order to overcome this deplorable state of affairs, which "as a whole" does not result "from any original backwardness,"[85] we need to reclaim "the historic initiative" or reassert "our generic human identity." But what exactly does this mean? As Towa points out, it means that we need to reaffirm

> our generic human identity—[which is] the power of conception, of signification, of thought and of implementation *[réalisation]*. Nothing, *a priori,* in our particular cultures is to be considered beyond critique. We pose as an absolute value, no element of our constituted culture nor the totality of this constituted [particular] culture, but the *generic human identity,* source of all constituted culture. Human generic identity, as the constituting activity of all culture, lies beneath all particular cultures because it is that which engenders them all.[86]

In other words, "generic human identity" is the ontological underpinning of being human, which is actualized in concrete ontic cultural-historical social formations.

Given the above, then, to overcome "underdevelopment" or dependence is to develop, which can only mean to reclaim our creative capacity and freedom as human beings in asserting—and concretely producing—the particular character and accent of our lived humanity. It is for this reason that, as Robert Bernasconi has noted, "European-style"[87] development theory cannot help in ameliorating our situation. This is precisely because, in its philosophy of history, it presupposes our destruction and bondage as a prerequisite for development, conceived of globally and in a unitary manner. In the guise of development it, thus, perpetuates the very "underdevelopment" it purports to overcome.

The notion of "endogenous development," however, need not necessarily be seen as only a parasitic negative-deconstructive critique "short-circuiting the European perspective to which it nevertheless remains inextricably tied."[88] If conceived in terms of Cabral's notion of a "return to the source"—explored in section II of this chapter—it has an open-ended critical reconstructive edge, in the manner of experimentally exploring what is possible against the negative backdrop of the Eurocentric model.[89] What is called for, then, is not "to resolve the problem,"[90] whatever that might mean, but to cultivate an open, released, and concurrently critical stance.[91] For, as Chinua Achebe has noted, science, technology, development, and so on are not "an assemblage of artefacts . . . but a particular attitude of mind,"[92] a stance resolutely open to the concrete historical possibilities of our own lived "generic human identity."

Fanon concludes *Les Damnés de la terre* with a simultaneous call to leave "old" Europe behind, stop aping it, and engage in the concrete inventing and creating of our own lived historicity: "Il faut inventer, il faut découvrir" [We must invent, we must discover].[93] To invent, the Latin *invenire,* here means to come upon ourselves, to discover ourselves; for once "old" Europe is left behind—once we see "European-style development" for what it is—we are then left to our own devices: "our generic human identity."

But to heed Fanon requires that we destructure the metaphysical constraints (universalism?) that have held us, and still hold us, captive. Thus, if one looks further behind the myopic hilarity that one finds behind the question "African philosophy?!" one comes across various theoretic efforts focused on the self-articulation of the emancipatory possibilities of the continent—beyond the hegemonic confines of the West.

6

The Heritage of the Idea:
Violence, Counterviolence, and the Negated

David Barsamian: But it is political.

Edward W. Said: Only in one sense: it is a politics against the reading of literature which would denude it and emasculate what in the literature is profoundly contested.

David Barsamian: But as a Teacher you're making certain choices.

Edward W. Said: Of course. We all do. I wouldn't deny that. It's a choice that proposes a different reading of these classics. I don't by any means say it's the only reading. I just say it's a relevant reading, and its the one that hasn't been addressed. I certainly don't intend to impose, because I think academic freedom is central to the issue, my reading on students and tell them if you don't read it this way you're failing the course. Quite the contrary. I want to provoke new and refreshing investigations of these texts in ways which will have them read more skeptically, more inquiringly, more searchingly. That's the point.

—The Pen and the Sword [1]

The theme of this chapter is the violence of the Idea and the counterviolence of those subjected to the "civilizing" ferocity of its implementation. In keeping with Edward W. Said's usage, by the term *Idea* I mean the "idea which dignifies pure force with arguments drawn from science, morality, ethics, and a *general philosophy.*" [2] For, as Father Placide Tempels has accurately noted, it is this "general philosophy" or Idea, which he refers to as "our civilizing mission"—in the variegated articulation of its core Eurocentric bias—that justifies "our occupation of the lands of uncivilized peoples." [3]

The task of this chapter is to explore the violent legacy of the Idea *(Idée),* [4] articulated by the iconic historical thinkers of the modern European philosophical tradition. By "iconic historical thinkers" I mean philosophers whose social, ethical, political, and historical reflections constitute the staple of most undergraduate and graduate programs in critical theory and continental philosophy: Immanuel Kant, G. W. F. Hegel, and Karl Marx. [5]

What I propose, then, is an explorative indication of how, in the iconic thinkers of the European tradition of philosophy, the violence of European expansion is authorized and sanctioned by the speculative fig leaf of the Idea.[6] It is the breaching of this sanctuary—the holy of holies of European thought—that gives our exploration its political edge. For what I am proposing is "profoundly contested"[7] by the orthodox reading of these iconic thinkers which, in the accepted rendition, presents them as thinkers of the possibility of human freedom in history.

I

For these thinkers, as for metaphysical thinking as a whole, the speculative labor of thought—in the realm of politics and history—is aimed at articulating the possibility of a peaceful and civil existence, given the strife and violence of actually existing historical societies. The aim, as much as possible, is to curtail violence and actualize the rationality of the real. In this regard, as Adriaan T. Peperzak correctly points out, "Plato still shape[s] the patterns of our thoughts, he also continues to offer guidance to all friends of *sophia,* especially to the young of mind and heart."[8] Indeed, as we shall see, in this "guidance"—and through its guise—Plato offers assistance not only to "all friends of sophia" but to a great deal more that is excused by and yet is contrary to any coherent notion of sophia.

As is well known, the key concern that animated Plato's thinking, in the realm of the political, was the question of a rationally ordered society. As he tells us,

> Hence I was forced to say in praise of the correct philosophy that it affords a vantage point from which we can discern in all cases what is just for communities and for individuals, and that accordingly the human race will not see better days until either the stock of those who rightly and genuinely follow philosophy acquire political authority, or else the class who have political control be led by some dispensation of providence to become real philosophers.[9]

The father of the tradition is concerned with the "vantage point from which to discern in all cases what is just for communities and individuals" so as to enable "the human race . . . better days." Plato thinks himself above the fray, and so inaugurates what Hannah Arendt has aptly described as the "old dream" of "Western metaphysics . . . of a timeless, spaceless, suprasensuous realm as the proper" domain of philosophy.[10] It is this epistemically untenable position that institutes the point of origin of Plato's thinking. This same position, as we shall see, permeates, in variegated ways, the modern European metaphysical tradition.

As H. D. F. Kitto tells us, in the dawn of Western history, the Greeks had divided humankind into Hellenes and barbarians.[11] Thus, in speaking of and for the "human race" as a whole, Plato does so in full awareness of what is and is not Greek. Assuming this distinction as an unquestioned given, Plato insists that the republic—the ideal state of "better days" for "the human race" as a whole—is to be strictly a Greek state.[12] What, then, of the barbarian?

In articulating the Idea *(eidos)* of such a state, Plato does not rule out violence. As is well known, those who construct the Idea, in "words,"[13] do not shy from the necessity and use of violence. In fact, based on this distinction, Plato argues that dispute among Greeks is civil strife and ought to be based on self-restraint and civility. Conflict with barbarians, on the other hand, is war properly speaking. For the barbarian is the legitimate prey of enslavement and pillage.[14] What, then, of the "human race" as a whole?

Let us listen to the master ventriloquist in his projected voices—Glaucon and Socrates:

> [G] I, he said, agree that our citizens ought to deal with their Greek opponents on this wise, while treating barbarians as Greeks now treat Greeks.
> [S] Shall we lay down this law also, then, for our guardians, that they are not to lay waste the land or burn the houses?
> [G] Let us so decree, he said, and assume that this and our preceding prescriptions are right.[15]

What are these "preceding prescriptions"? Greeks should not enslave Greeks and should refrain from doing what usually is done by victors to vanquished in any conflict that involves Greeks. Greeks should guard against being enslaved by barbarians[16] and treat them, the barbarians, the way "Greeks now treat Greeks." Enslavement, pillage, laying the land waste, exterminating women and children—the basic theme of Euripides' *The Trojan Women*—are all legitimate practices in conflict with barbarians. On these points, Glaucon and Socrates are unequivocally agreed.

But why should Greeks refrain from such heinous practices among themselves? These detestable practices should be refrained from, according to Plato, not because they are odious per se but because, and insofar as, they endanger Greece by exposing her to barbarian enslavement. Again, let us listen in on Glaucon and Socrates:

> [S] First, in the matter of making slaves of the defeated, do you think it right for Greeks to reduce Greek cities to slavery, or rather that, so far as they are able, they should not suffer any other city to do so, but should accustom Greeks to spare Greeks, foreseeing the danger of enslavement by the barbarians?
> [G] Sparing them is wholly and altogether the better, said he.[17]

In addition to the above, this pan-Hellenic solidarity—grounded on fear of and against the barbarians—is to be cemented by the fact that Hellas is "their nurse and mother" and is to be treated accordingly.[18] The motherland and/or fatherland, whichever one prefers, is sacred and inviolable!

Plato continues,

[S] And won't they be philhellenes, lovers of Greeks, and will they not regard all Greece as their own and not renounce their part in the holy places common to all Greeks?
[G] Most certainly.[19]

In all of the above, then, what is the effect or function of the distinction between Greek and non-Greek? This distinction effectively sanctions, and serves as a sanctuary for, bestiality and violence. Against whom? The violence is against those that have been very conveniently and neatly designated as strangers, outsiders, aliens, barbarians, that is, the bestial.

As Plato has Socrates say, "I affirm that the Hellenic race is friendly to itself and akin, and foreign and alien to the barbarian." To this Glaucon replies, "Rightly."[20] Or, if one prefers Grube's translation, "You are right."[21] Thus, the fear of bestiality effectively authorizes bestiality! But how does this distinction actually work?

As should be clear by now, this distinction starts out by proposing a position that is synchronously universal and particular. It is universal in that it addresses and speaks for the "human race" in toto. And yet it is particular, for the Idea is, properly speaking, Greek. Plato's "vantage point from which we can discern in all cases what is just,"[22] precisely because of the way it is formulated tacitly, negates the lived particularity within which it is articulated and elevates itself to the status of universality. In other words, it operates in terms of a *false double negation*.[23] In implicitly negating its own lived situatedness and/or particularity, it claims the status of humanity as such, while synchronously, the non-Greek, the barbarian—labeled and designated as such by the Greek—is negated and, in the name of humanity, relegated to a subhuman status. This gesture of double negation is false in that in its claim to universality it surreptitiously negates the Other, whose particularity has been labeled and reduced to the barbarous, and, in the same act, elevates its own particularity to the status of the universal.

Now the question that needs to be asked is, Is this just an idiosyncratic aspect of Plato's thinking,[24] or does it carry over and ground the modern heritage of European philosophy? In answering this question in the affirmative, this chapter will show how this false gesture of double negation is replicated and sustained—in differing idioms—by the central historical thinkers of the modern tradition of European philosophy: Kant, Hegel, and Marx.

II

In "What Is Enlightenment?" Michel Foucault, commenting on Kant's classic piece "What Is Enlightenment?" (1784), remarks that Kant's "use of the word 'mankind' *(Menschheit)*" is rather problematic and goes on to ask, "Are we to understand that the entire human race is caught up in the process of Enlightenment? In that case, we must imagine the Enlightenment as a historical change that affects the political and social existence of all people on the face of the earth. Or are we to understand that it involves a change affecting what constitutes the humanity of human beings?"[25] By postulating an "either/or," Foucault bypasses the crucial question of whose humanity is at stake in the project of rational self-liberation articulated by Kant. For as Kant tells us, his concern is with "the totality of men united socially on earth into peoples."[26] And simultaneously, as Foucault correctly points out, Kant is also concerned with the speculative issue of "what constitutes the humanity of human beings" as such.

It is precisely because Kant conflates these two issues that his conception of Enlightenment has a domineering/violent effect in "respect to others."[27] But why should this conflation have such an effect? Foucault neither pursues nor responds to this question precisely because he disconnects what Kant conflates and, thus, dissolves the source of the problem.

In fact, Kant does not make a distinction between the historical/empirical and speculative aspects of his formulation regarding "mankind" (Menschheit). As we shall see, it is the speculative effort to sketch out "the process of Enlightenment" as it affects "the humanity of human beings" conflated with the historical/empirical concern with "the entire human race" or "all people on the face of the earth" that makes for this domineering and violent effect in "respect to others." It is, in other words, "the 'transcendentalization' of the historical fact of the *Aufklärung*"[28] that allows Kant to project/impose as the destiny of humanity—if need be by violence—the singular ideals, hopes, and aspirations of his own age and culture.

To be sure, Kant was not a person devoid of sympathy or compassion for non-European peoples. In "Perpetual Peace" (1795) he is quite disturbed by the inhumanity of civilized commercial European states in their dealings and contacts with non-European peoples. In the section in which he discusses "universal hospitality" as the law of "world citizenship" and after noting how the "ship and the camel (the desert ship)" bring people together and can foster "peaceable relations," he makes the following remarkable statement:

> But to this perfection compare the inhospitable actions of the civilized and especially of the commercial states of our part of the world. The injustice which they show to the lands and peoples they visit (which is equivalent to conquering them) is carried by them to terrifying lengths. America, the lands inhabited by the Negro, the Spice Islands, the Cape, etc., were at the time of their discovery considered by these civilized intruders as lands without owners, for they counted the inhabitants as nothing.[29]

The same Kant, however, also writes that "if the happy inhabitants of Tahiti, never visited [conquered] by more civilized nations, were destined to live in their quiet indolence for thousands of centuries," one could not give a satisfactory answer to the question "why they bothered to exist at all, and whether it would not have been just as well that this island should have been occupied by happy sheep and cattle as by happy men engaged in mere pleasure?"[30]

The force of Kant's rhetorical question is directed at emphasizing what he calls "the value of existence itself,"[31] which is not, in his view, manifested in the placid, sedate, or idle pursuit of "mere pleasure." It is, as Kant is well aware, when Europeans "visit (which is equivalent to conquering . . .)"[32] such places as Tahiti that the indigenous form of life (which he depicts as "mere pleasure") is radically impeached and replaced by what is viewed as proper to "the value of existence itself." What, then, is "the value of existence itself"?

In "Conjectural Beginning of Human History" (1786), freely utilizing the Genesis story—that is, the Judeo-Christian myth of creation and origins—Kant lists the four likely steps by which reason extracts man from instinct and his original abode in the garden of paradise. The fourth "and final step which reason took," he writes, to raise man "altogether above community with animals," occurred when man realized that he himself was the "true end of nature";[33] "The first time he ever said to the sheep, 'nature has given you the skin you wear for my use, not yours'; the first time he ever took that skin and put it upon himself ([Genesis], 3:21)—that time he became aware of the way in which his nature privileged and raised him above all animals."[34] In his remarks on the above, on the next page, leaving allegory and sheepish examples aside, Kant states bluntly that reason separates man from instinct/nature by establishing total dominion over the natural realm: "Man's departure from that paradise which his reason represents as the first abode of his species was nothing but the transition from an uncultured, merely animal condition to the state of humanity, from bondage to instinct to rational control—in a word, from the tutelage of nature to the state of humanity."[35] In other words, those whose humanness—by its lack of differentiation from and dominion over nature—resembles the placid and carefree existence of sheep, cattle, and animals in general are still within the realm of instinct and have not yet ascended to "the state of freedom" that reason makes possible. It is important to emphasize that by *reason* is here understood the instrumental and calculating control—"rational control"—of the natural environment and of the human person, as a being of nature, with the possibility of rational freedom in contradistinction to the "lawless freedom" of "savages."[36] It is important to note further that Kant sees a similarity between the Tahitians (and non-European humanity by extension)[37] and sheep because—at least, if one is to judge by the illustrations he uses—sheep, for him, typify the paradigmatic example of a passive resource to be exploited.

Thus, for Kant, the "value of existence itself," which is ontologically or metaphysically proper to human life, is manifested in the rational control of nature: Dominion over nature, or the lack thereof, is thus the truth of the "value of existence itself." In other words, Kant cannot be candid in his critique of the imperialistic practices of European states—what he labels their "inhospitable actions"—because he himself thinks that the Tahitians are "nothing," that is, mere sheep.[38]

Kant's speculative discourse systematically substantiates this very "inhospitable" attitude in explicating the hidden workings of the "unsocial sociability" of man's nature.[39] In other words, humanity achieves greatness not as a result of its own inclinations but by the secret design of nature. "Man," Kant tells us, "wishes concord. . . . He wishes to live comfortably and pleasantly; Nature wills that he should be plunged from sloth and passive [sheepish] contentment into labor and trouble in order that he may find means of extricating himself from them."[40] For this purpose it has devised human nature as inherently antagonistic—it is social, and yet it also inclines to isolation and conflict: "This opposition it is which awakens all his powers, brings him to conquer his inclination to laziness and, propelled by vainglory, lust for power, and avarice, to achieve a rank among his fellows whom he cannot tolerate but from whom he cannot withdraw."[41] It is in this manner that, for Kant, the first steps are taken from "barbarism" to "culture," and gradually by "continued enlightenment the beginnings are laid" through which "a society of men driven together by their natural feelings" constitute "a moral whole."[42] Otherwise, says Kant, "men, good-natured as the sheep they herd, would hardly reach a higher worth than their beasts; they would not fill the empty place in creation by achieving their end, which is rational nature."[43]

The reader should note that "the empty place in creation" and Kant's earlier analogous formulation "the value of existence itself"[44] are fulfilled or actualized by "rational nature," that is, the ratio at work in the instrumental control of nature and of human life. And this, in turn, is accomplished by the "unsocial sociability" of man "propelled by vainglory, lust for power, and avarice," which "awaken all his powers." Thus, Kant extols nature for imprinting this basic aggressiveness in man: "Thanks be to nature, then, for the incompatibility, for heartless competitive vanity, for insatiable desire to possess and rule! Without them, all the excellent natural capacities of humanity would forever sleep, undeveloped. Man wishes concord; but nature knows better what is good for the race; she wills discord."[45] Indeed, without "heartless competitive vanity" or an "insatiable desire to possess and rule," what Cornel West appropriately refers to as "the age of Europe" would never have come to pass.[46] But then it should be noted—contra Kant—that the imperialistic attitude of European states in their dealings with the non-European world is driven precisely by this ontic-historical antagonistic disposition that he ontologizes and yet deplores.

Kant cannot have it both ways. He cannot on the one hand extol and impute to nature—and hence ontologize—the violent propensities of European history and simultaneously condemn the effects of these very drives. Thus, violent conquest and imperialist expansion are part of the foresight and design of nature! And all of this is to be understood in terms of "the destination of the human race in general, [which] is perpetual progress, and its perfection is a simple, but in all respects very useful, Idea of the goal to which . . . we have to direct our efforts."[47] As noted in the exordium to this chapter, this Idea (Idée) is the imperious notion of European superiority with which Kant begins, constructs, and concludes his historico-philosophic reflections as a whole. It is in this manner that his thinking sanctions the violence of European conquest.

III

As is well known, for Hegel the difference that marks off the Negro African from humanity proper is his immediacy and undifferentiated immersion in nature. It is this lack—this "naturalness"—that places the Negro beyond the pale of history.[48] Africa, as Hegel tells us in *The Philosophy of History* (1830), "is the Unhistorical, Undeveloped Spirit, still involved in the conditions of mere nature."[49] Regarding such a *Geist* (spirit), lacking in all that is human, says Hegel, "we may conclude slavery to have been the occasion of the increase of human feeling among the Negroes."[50] Thus, for Hegel, enslavement humanizes the Negro African!

In the *Philosophy of Right* (1821), after detailing the endemic socioeconomic problems of "civil society"—European modernity—Hegel presents colonial expansion as the only acceptable solution to these endemic problems, which simultaneously and propitiously actualizes the Idea on a global scale.[51] In this scenario, for Hegel, the "rights of barbarians" are not equal to those of members of civilized nations. Civilized nations, precisely because they are civilized, can justifiably treat the "autonomy" of barbarians "as only a formality,"[52] for it is the "absolute right of the Idea to step into existence in clear-cut laws and objective institutions" that can justifiably be secured through "force and wrong."[53] In other words, "lower" peoples or "barbarians" are the legitimate prey of conquest, in the service of the Idea.[54]

Thus, "to him who looks upon the world rationally," says Hegel, "the world in its turn presents a rational aspect."[55] This, needless to say, is the rationality of violence or its surreptitious rationalization. For behind these remarks, which endorse the violence of slavery and colonial conquest, as required by the default of humanity in the Negro, one finds the gratuitous—because rationally unwarranted and unwarrantable—Idea of European superiority. For "every stage is the Idea, but earlier stages contain it only in rather an abstract form."[56] In other words, that which is "earlier" and/or undeveloped (i.e., "abstract") is designated as such by that which is "later" and/or developed. But on what grounds is the "later" and/or developed certified in its mature status or concreteness?

Hegel elevates to the status of reason the cultural and historical prejudices of the Europe of his day, that is, the Idea. Prejudices that, to this day, "still permeate philosophy, as well as being instruments in contemporary world politics in programs of economic and social development."[57] In other words, as Marcien Towa has pointedly noted,

Western imperialism [colonialism] finds one of its most elaborate ideological expressions in the Hegelian philosophy of history according to which the modern civiliza-

tion of Europe constitutes the universal synthesis of all the values produced by humanity in the course of its long history. The occident is thus proclaimed the Absolute of
the world in front of which all other peoples are without rights. In it the Spirit of the
world is completely developed and determined: "the principle is realized and, as a
consequence, time is complete." The other civilizations have nothing of value to offer
Europe, the universal heritage of humanity, which it does not already possess, as a
surpassed moment of the historic development of Spirit. [I]n front of . . . Europe other
civilizations and other peoples are without value and can thus be reduced by it to the
condition of simple instruments. . . . Under cover of this absolutisation of itself, the
Occident perversely indulges itself, with a good conscience, *in the destruction of other
civilizations across the world.*[58]

This systematic violence, or in Towa's phrase, "the destruction of other civilizations," is directed, vindicated, and justified by Europe's own "absolutisation of
itself" as "the universal heritage of humanity" as such, that is, the Idea actualized.
Thus, imperious nineteenth-century Europe's self-conceit is palmed off—in the
guise of the Idea—as transcendental wisdom! In this regard, Hegel's thinking "can
be seen as the fulfillment of the sketch for a philosophical account of universal history proposed by Kant."[59]

IV

Staying within the overall direction of Hegel's and Kant's viewpoint, for Marx the
ancient Greeks—to whom the West traces its cultural/intellectual origins—are the
true archaic origin of humanity. "There are," Marx writes, "rude children and pre-
cocious children. Many of the ancient peoples belong to this category. The Greeks
were normal Children."[60] Such remarks are quite revealing. Marx, a European,
judges his ancestry relative to other ancestries by the standards of European culture and concludes that the "Greeks were normal" as opposed to Other archaic peoples who are, thus, judged to be less than the norm!

Indeed, as Anwar Abdel Melik has noted, "the 'normal man,' it is understood"
in the kind of thinking exhibited by Kant, Hegel, and Marx, is "the European man
of the historical period, that is, since Greek antiquity."[61] It is because he sees it as
the avenue through which this norm will be established on a global scale that Marx
supports colonial conquest. As Marx notes in the *Manifesto,* the capitalist mode of
production—a peculiar product of European history—reveals "what man's activity can bring about"; it creates the privileged historical and cultural context in
which man is "compelled to face with sober senses his *real* conditions of life and
his relations with his kind."[62]

What colonialism spreads globally is the "real conditions of" human "life" in
contrast to the unreality of non-European existence. Indeed, for Marx, the "bourgeois period of history has to create the material basis of the new world," which
is "the development of the productive powers of man and the transformation of

material production into a scientific domination of natural agencies."[63] And in order to accomplish this it has to fulfill a "double mission," the destruction of non-European civilizations along with the simultaneous "laying of the material foundation of Western society" globally.[64]

In other words, for Marx, in terms of the destiny of humanity, colonialism is the "unconscious tool of history" that will prepare "mankind [to] fulfill its destiny."[65] This it will do by extricating precapitalist non-European humanity—as he tells us in *Capital,* volume 1—from its "immaturity,"[66] which is manifested as its immersion in nature. For, as Frederick Engels puts it, the mastery of nature "is the final [and] essential distinction between man and other animals."[67] Thus, colonialism is the necessary precondition for the proper humanization of the non-European world.

Indeed, as Marx remarks of India under British tutelage, "a fresh class is springing up . . . imbued with European science,"[68] and the Indians "will not reap the fruits of the new elements . . . scattered among them by the British . . . till in Great Britain the now ruling classes shall have been supplanted by the industrial proletariat."[69] The destiny of humanity is in the hands of the West and the Westernized évolué. Everything, for Marx, is to be subsumed within the globalized history of Europe!

V

It is important to note that behind and beyond these slightly different perspectives of Kant, Hegel, and Marx lies the *singular* bias or Idea that European humanity is, properly speaking, isomorphic with the humanity of the human as such. This Idea, grounded in the false double negation initiated by Plato, is the foundation and base of the modern tradition of Western philosophy. In this speculative schema, the colonial destruction of non-European humanity is seen as laying the groundwork for the global actualization of the ultimate value of human existence as such: the calculative control of nature.

The overall speculative perspective articulated by these icons is, thus, "a philosophy of terrorism [i.e., of violence]" to the extent that, as Gianni Vattimo has noted, *"it takes to its extreme consequence* the idea that human history has an absolute norm, a final value to be realized; the individuals or the classes [or nations] who feel they are (based on evidence which, in the final analysis, is intuitive) the bearers *[portatori]* of this value, acquire the right of life or death over all the others."[70] As noted earlier, this is what Towa refers to as Europe's "absolutisation of itself" in terms of which it then "indulges itself, with a good conscience, in the destruction of other civilizations" and in so doing sees itself as "the universal heritage of humanity."[71] For as Cornelius Castoriadis puts it, "there is . . . no superiority, nor inferiority to the West. There is simply a fact: namely that the Earth has been unified by means of Western violence."[72]

The speculative discourse of and on the Idea is, thus, nothing more than a rather lame "pretext" for unmitigated global violence,[73] a violence that effectively cripples the colonized's subjectivity,[74] which it subjugates. How so? "Pushed by the logic of domination, the imperialist powers have combated and destroyed in the societies of the periphery all the *forces—peoples, institutions, beliefs*—opposed to bondage, that is to say, in general, all that was most healthy in these societies."[75] In all that it sanctions, the net effect of the Idea is to negate the lived historicity/humanity of the colonized. The defensive counterviolence of the negated, on the other hand, is aimed at the protection of life and of human dignity, in the differing historical actualities of its actualization.

But what does this mean concretely? The historian A. J. Barker has preserved for us the dying words of an anonymous African anticolonial fighter:

> One captured Ethiopian with a bullet wound in the head who was interrogated by the Italians obviously had not long to live. But he faced his captors with dignity. "Who are you?" he was asked. "The commander of a thousand men *[ye-shí aléká]*." "Why don't you lie down on that stretcher? The Italians do not harm their prisoners." "I prefer to die on my feet. We swore to our King that we would capture your positions, or die in the attempt. We have not won, but we have died. Look. . . !" And the Ethiopian pointed to the valley littered with corpses.[76]

The stern courage of these words is not sanctioned by or derived from an Idea—a metaphysical bias/belief. It is the expression of life defending itself. A reader acquainted with the struggle for recognition in Hegel's descriptive account of conflict in the *Phenomenology of Spirit* or with Heidegger's depiction of "freedom towards death" in *Being and Time* cannot fail to notice that the words of this African anticolonial fighter verbalize the lived experience of "the consciousness that refuses to barter, or even contemplate the possibility of bartering, its concrete ethical life—i.e., freedom—for biological existence."[77]

Far from being immersed in and undifferentiated from nature, as Hegel and Marx believed, or being no better than sheep, as Kant maintained, the humanity of those negated by the metaphysically sanctioned violence of European conquest is itself a specific actualization of human existence that does not arrogate to itself the hubris of cultural-historical solipsism. Faced with an unresolvable contradiction focused on religion, for example, the Elders in Chinua Achebe's *Things Fall Apart* state, "We cannot leave the matter in his [i.e., the missionary's] hands because he does not understand our customs, just as we do not understand his. We say he is foolish because he does not know our ways, and perhaps he says we are foolish because we do not know his. Let him go away."[78] But colonizing Europe did not "go away"! Possessed of the wisdom/hubris that its own existence was coterminous with human existence per se, it could not countenance the existence of differing—and equally legitimate—modes of human life. For its "civilizing mission"—its own self-serving Idea of its place in the world—categorically sanctioned the "occupation of the lands of uncivilized peoples."[79]

The counterviolence of the negated or "uncivilized," on the other hand—the

dying Ethiopian or the Elders of Umuofia—is aimed at restoring a reciprocal bal-
ance of recognition between differing and/or conflicting modes of human life. In
this regard, Antonio Gramsci—whose thinking does not fall within *"la fallacia
platonica"*[80]—writes,

> Then one day the rumor spreads: a student has killed the English governor of the
> Indies, or: the Italians have been defeated at Dogali, or: the Boxers have exterminated
> the European missionaries; and then horror-stricken old Europe curses against the bar-
> barians, against the uncivilized, and a new crusade is undertaken against those unfor-
> tunate people.
>
> And notice: the Europeans have had their own oppressors and have fought bloody
> struggles to liberate themselves, and now they erect status and marble memorials to
> their liberators, to their heroes, and they exalt to national religion the cult of those
> who died for the country. But don't say to the Italians that the Austrians came to
> bring us civilization: even the marble columns would protest. We of course, have
> gone forth to extend civilization, and in fact now those people love us and thank
> heaven for their fortune. But we know. . . . Truth instead consists in the insatiable
> craving that everyone has of milking their equals, of snatching from them what lit-
> tle they have been able to save through privation. Wars are fought for commerce,
> not for civilization.[81]

The simplicity of the above observations hides a very deep human sensibility,
a sensibility that has eluded and still eludes the thinking of most European philosophers. This sensibility is open to the stern courage and the reciprocity in recognition out of which the counterviolence of the negated originates. For in reaffirming
that war is motivated by "commerce"—an observation made by Plato in the
Republic—Gramsci asserts the essential human equality of the aggressor and the
aggressed and refuses Plato's distinction between Greek and non-Greek, a distinction that, as we have seen, the icons of the modern tradition reassert as that
between Europe and the rest of us, that is, the civilized and the uncivilized.

This recognition of the humanity of the Other exposes the hypocrisy of those
who conquer in the name of civilization and refuse—in their turn—the violence
of the Idea that drives the logic of civilizing conquest. For Gramsci, this hypocrisy
undermines the sense and meaning of the freedom of the colonizers and makes of
their "marble memorials" so many stones! On the other hand, the violence of the
colonized—the killing of the "English governor of the Indies," the Italian defeat
at Dogali, or the extermination of "European missionaries"—is seen for what it is,
a possible human reaction to an imposed condition of prolonged violence, that is,
an inhuman condition.

The counterviolence of the colonized is an effort aimed at redeeming a squandered humanity, a humanity squandered by the violence of the Idea. For the rest,
the colonized in their struggle do not justify violence, they only strive to live up
to the requirements of their "being-history." As Cabral has noted, "Naturally, we
are not defending the armed fight. Maybe I deceive people, but I am not a great

defender of the armed fight. I am myself very conscious of the sacrifices demanded by the armed fight. It is a violence against even our own people. But it is not our invention—it is not our cool decision; it is a *requirement of history*."[82] In other words, it is a "requirement" of our human existence affirming itself and re-entering the realm of the historical.

Conclusion: The Postcolonial Sensibility

Sensibility is the capacity to be affected. To lack a sensibility is to be deficient in something. Children with an impoverished upbringing do not have an appreciation for, or are not affected by, the finer things of life. A cloistered upbringing, by shutting out the "world," cultivates a person's religiosity. This receptivity is not, however, a preformed passive receptacle. It is not an empty container that precedes its contents; it is formed by the very contents that it receives. As Hans-Georg Gadamer puts it,

> Every single individual that raises himself out of his natural being to the spiritual finds in the language, customs and institutions of his people a pre-given body of material which, as in learning to speak, he has to make his own. Thus every individual is always engaged in the process of *Bildung* and in getting beyond his naturalness, inasmuch as the world into which he is growing is one that is humanly constituted through language and custom. Hegel emphasises that a people gives itself its existence in its world. It works out from itself and thus exteriorises what it is in itself.[1]

Indeed, but Gadamer (along with Hegel) presupposes—in describing the way an individual or a historical community "gives itself its existence in its world"—a homogeneous and autonomous self-standing historical community. What if generations of individuals raise themselves out of their "natural being to the spiritual" and experience the ethical life that nurtures their formation as a fractured in-between, an antagonistic world, that is, the unstable mélange of the ancestors and European modernity? For as Frantz Fanon has noted, "All colonized people—that is to say, all people in whose spirit is born an inferiority complex, by the burial of its local cultural originality—find themselves face to face with the language of the civilizing nation, that is to say, the metropolitan culture."[2] This is the "zone de non-être" in and through which, as we saw in chapter 1, self-estranged Western-ized Africa struggles to redeem itself. In so doing, "it works out of itself and thus exteriorises what it is in itself." But "what it is in itself" is not a self-standing homogeneous whole but an identity created in struggle, a pasticcio produced out of conflict, a sensibility that is the lived composite of antagonistic elements in need of a concrete synthesis.

As we saw in chapters 2 and 3 (in our discussion of W. E. B. Du Bois and African American slave narratives), the enslaved and their free descendants do not struggle to reclaim some true past fixed identity. Rather, their struggles are directed at reclaiming humanity within the ambient that has negated it. In freeing themselves their efforts contribute toward the humanizing of the very world that has dehumanized them. In this struggle what is articulated is, broadly speaking, a way of relating—that is, a sensibility—to the world that ontologically comprehends it as structured by and in our own involvements in the world.

In chapter 4, in critically exploring what Kwame Appiah has to say of African identity, and in chapter 5, in looking at the question of African philosophy, we saw that the critically self-reflective discourse of contemporary African philosophy is itself a moment in the concrete self-formative process of contemporary Africa. It is itself part of "the story" that, as Chinua Achebe has noted, we do not own, "the story that owns us and directs us . . . the thing that makes us different from cattle."[3] To be "different from cattle," to be human, then, means to be those beings that spin a web of being, a story, out of our own lived situatedness.

In one of his fragments, the ancient Greek philosopher Xenophanes tells us that, if cattle, horses, or lions "could draw," each species would make gods in their own image "in accordance with the form that each species itself possesses."[4] But then cattle would not be cattle anymore! For, unlike all other sentient forms of life, the human being is that form of life that is actualized within the ambient of a "story." The "story" forms our humanity by infusing it with the specific particularity of a culture/time in which we are born. Our humanity, in being formed in a dialectical manner, in turn actualizes the "story" in actively appropriating it.

This interplay of passive activity and active passivity constitutes in a dialectical manner the substantial actuality of a heritage or tradition. Thus, as Hegel puts it, "A people gives itself its existence in its world. It works out from itself and thus exteriorises what it is in itself." In appropriating this view from Hegel, Gadamer does so in order to suggest that, long before we engage in the critically detached process of theoretic understanding, we always already understand as and in the way our ambient or heritage gives us to understand. But what if our heritage is drastically marked, constituted, and formed by the violent globalization and superimposition of European modernity? For human existence is always—and necessarily—actualized within the lived heritage of a specific tradition.

I

The postcolonial sensibility originates in this globalization of Europe and the concomitant Westernization of non-European peoples who, on the one hand, have a grasp of the value of modern European civilization and, in the same breath, recognize the worth of that which was destroyed, and is being destroyed, by Euro-American expansion. It is in struggle—out of this recognition—that the imperious proclivities of European expansion have been curtailed. And in this process, the formerly enslaved and colonized have carved out for themselves a human heritage.

As Edward Said has noted, in 1914 Euro-America had under its direct control 85 percent of the globe.[5] Today, at the end of the century, we are beyond direct colonialism and blatant, officially sanctioned, segregationist racism. This propitious situation was the result, as Gianni Vattimo has correctly noted, of prolonged and bitter struggle:

> It is . . . understood that the actual crisis of the unitary conception of history, the consequent crisis of the idea of progress and the end of modernity, are not events determined only by theoretic transformations—the critique that 19th century historicism (idealistic, positivistic, Marxist, etc.) suffered on the level of ideas. Many more and diverse things have happened: the "primitive" peoples, labeled as such, and colonized by the Europeans in the name of having a right to a more "superior" and evolved civilization, have *rebelled* and *de facto* made problematic a unitary and centralized history. The European ideal of humanity has been exposed *[svelato]* as an ideal among others, not necessarily inferior, but which cannot, without violence, *pretend* to be equal to the true essence of the human being, of the human as such.[6]

Again, Vattimo writes, "In the United States of the last few decades minorities of every kind have taken the *word* [hanno preso la parola], cultures and sub-cultures of every kind have presented themselves on the stage of public opinion."[7] The rebellion of the colonized (African) and the word/voice of the formerly enslaved/dehumanized and presently marginalized (African American) have put in question de facto the validity of white or Euro-American supremacy and thus brought about this propitious situation. As we saw in chapters 2 and 3, by focusing on the struggle of former slaves and their descendants, and as we saw in chapters 4 and 5, by focusing on Africa, this struggle in overcoming domination simultaneously transforms the subjectivity imposed on the dominated as a condition of their domination. Thinking the process of this transformation is what I have termed the "postcolonial sensibility," a thinking formed and required by this propitious situation. And by "propitious situation" I mean our contemporary situation in which colonialism has been surpassed and yet, in most everything, the formerly colonized world is still dependent on its former colonizers. In like manner the descendants of slaves have emancipated themselves and achieved the status of "equal" citizenship, and yet they still suffer formal and informal forms of discrimination.

As Fanon noted in 1960, from the front lines of the African liberation struggle, the central theoretic problem that has faced Africa and, one might add, its Diaspora for quite some time, "the great danger that threatens Africa" and makes for backsliding and unpleasant surprises, "is the absence of ideology."[8] This, however, does not necessarily mean aligning one's theoretic perspective with pre-established ideological paradigms. It means thinking through the historic possibilities of the struggle in terms of its own lived specificity and the exigencies of quotidian existence that fuel its efforts.

In this perspective, the work of theory is not aimed at flattening the sense of events, in terms of pregiven master narratives, but at hermeneutically seeking out and elucidating the *possible* in the *actual* eventuation of lived existence. In and out of the concrete actualities of the present to seek a glimmer, the trace of a possible future—this is the task of theory. Or, as Amilcar Cabral noted in 1972, ideology does not "necessarily mean that you have to define whether you are [a] communist, socialist, or something like this. To have ideology is to know what you want [and what is possible] in your own *condition.*"[9] Indeed, as far back as 1956 Aimé Césaire had keenly observed—against the hegemonic and crassly reductionist proclivities of the European Left—the need for such a theoretic stance solidly grounded on "knowing what you want and what is possible in your own condition."

In his *Lettre à Maurice Thorez*—endorsed by all the differing political perspectives and personalities that then constituted *Présence Africaine*—Césaire categorically affirms, for the formerly enslaved and colonized, the right to reclaim and re-enter the realm of historical existence on their own terms.[10] It is only in this manner and given this "knowing what we want in our own condition" that we can properly own up to, value, and thus consolidate—on its own terms—the de facto heritage, the struggle and sacrifice, that has made possible for us the philosophical and political space within which we theorize.

In other words, it is necessary to theoretically dismantle all that was built on and, thus, mantled and buttressed by the grounding and key assumptions of European supremacy/modernity.

In this effort, theoretic work would concretely partake of the process of reintroducing humanity into history, the process through which humanity reinvents itself. For the de facto situation of the present calls for—as completion and counterpart—a de jure theoretic unfrocking of the mantle of dominance. God is dead! But his shadow still endures: "We still have to vanquish his shadow, too."[11]

In this shadowy combat, in order to minimize backsliding, it is necessary, *on its own terms,* to enunciate the stance of this world-shaking *rebellion* and *voice.* This is what I have labeled the postcolonial sensibility. My efforts in this study have been focused on exploring this perspective, that of the "formerly colonized [and enslaved], the oppressed, that . . . struggle for more justice and equality,"[12] as it arises out of the lived and "effective-history" of their heritage.

Notes

INTRODUCTION

1. Frantz Fanon, *Les Damnés de la terre* (Paris: François Maspero, 1974), p. 226; and *The Wretched of the Earth*, trans. Constance Farrington (New York: Grove Press, 1963), p. 157.

2. David Diop, "Afrique" ("Africa"), in *Négritude: Black Poetry from Africa and the Caribbean*, ed. and trans. Norman R. Shapiro (London: October House Ltd., 1970), p. 145. Aimé Césaire, *Return to My Native Land* (Baltimore: Penguin Books, 1970).

3. Plato, "Phaedo," #61b, trans. G. M. A. Grube, *Plato: Five Dialogues* (Indianapolis: Hackett Publishing Co., 1981), p. 97.

4. Kwame Gyekye, *African Cultural Values* (Philadelphia and Accra: Sankofa Publishing Co., 1996), p. xiii. Marcien Towa has conclusively demonstrated this point in *L'Idée d'une philosophie négro-africaine* (Yaoundé: Editions Clé, 1979), chap. 2, sec. 3.

5. There are, today, in sub-Saharan Africa quite a few governments that, in recognition of this failure, have made the cornerstone of all their efforts the systematic effort to transform their societies into viable politico-economic autonomous countries. On this hopeful note, see Philip Gourevitch, "Continental Shift," *The New Yorker,* 4 August 1997, pp. 42–55. To be sure, these countries labor in a world dominated and managed, more and more crassly, by the single overbearing power of the Occident, the United States. (In this regard, Ethiopia's belligerence toward Eritrea and its policy of total war, over minor border disputes, cannot be seen or understood apart from the overbearing presence of the United States in the region.) But, even in this context, one can hope for some "relative autonomy" in spite of the villainous machinations of this single super power. For a concise overview of these machinations, see Gore Vidal, "The Last Empire," *Vanity Fair* 447 (November 1997), pp. 219–76. For a sense of the aspirations of the struggles of the late 1950s and early 1960s, see Kwame Nkrumah, "Extract from the Midnight Pronouncement of Independence," from his midnight speech on the occasion of Ghana's independence—5–6 March 1957—in *Revolutionary Path* (London: Panaf Books Ltd., 1980), pp. 120–21.

6. Kwasi Wiredu, *Cultural Universals and Particulars* (Bloomington and Indianapolis: Indiana University Press, 1996). For an engaging review of this book, see E. C. Eze, "What Are Cultural Universals? *Cultural Universals and Particulars* by Kwasi Wiredu," *African Philosophy* 11, no. 1 (June 1998), pp. 73–82.

7. To my knowledge, this analogy was first noted by Aimé Césaire, *Présence Africaine*, nos. 8–10 (June–November 1956), pp. 225–26.

8. H. Jack Geiger, "The Real World of Race," *The Nation* 265, no. 18 (1 December 1997), pp. 27–29.

9. Robert Gooding-Williams, *Reading Rodney King* (New York and London: Routledge, 1993), specifically "Look, a Negro!," pp. 157–77.

10. Cornel West, *Race Matters* (Boston: Beacon Press, 1993), specifically chap. 2.

11. For thinking that moves along similar lines, see Lucius Outlaw, *On Race and Philosophy* (New York: Routledge, 1996).

12. Hans-Georg Gadamer, *Truth and Method* (New York: Crossroad Publishing Co., 1982), p. 268.

13. Okonda w'oleko Okolo, *Pour une philosophie de la culture et du développement: Recherches d'herméneutique et de praxis africaines* (Kinshasa: Presses Universitaires du Zaire, 1986), p. 45. It should be noted that the term *scientific (scientifique)*, in the way that Okolo makes use of it—or in general the way it is used by francophone and German thinkers—has nothing to do with the natural sciences as such but, rather, refers to rigorous theoretic or scientific work in any field of study.

14. On this point, see Antonio Gramsci, *Quaderni del carcere: Edizione critica dell'Istituto Gramsci, a cura di Valentino Gerratana* (Torino, Italy: Giulio Einaudi, 1975), p. 1376.

15. Towa, *L'Idée d'une philosophie négro-africaine*, p. 50.

16. This question has become rather "topical" as of late; on this, see *W. E. B. Du Bois on Race and Culture*, ed. B. W. Bell, E. R. Grosholz, and J. B. Stewart (New York and London: Routledge, 1996).

17. Appiah deserves such "attention" precisely because his views, on this question, are becoming more and more the established means of undermining any sense of black or pan-African identity that is not racially tainted.

18. For a similar position, see Marcien Towa, "Propositions sur l'identité culturelle," *Présence Africaine* 109 (1st Quarter, 1979), pp. 82–91; and *L'Idée d'une philosophie négro-africaine*.

19. Edward W. Said, *The Pen and the Sword* (Monroe, Maine: Common Courage Press, 1994), p. 75.

20. Okolo, *Pour une philosophie de la culture et du développement*, p. 46.

21. Ibid., p. 44.

22. Cornelius Castoriadis, interview by Florian Rötzer, *Conversation with French Philosophers* (Atlantic Highlands, N.J.: Humanities Press, 1995), p. 31.

23. Ibid.

24. Søren Kierkegard, struggling against the hypocrisy—as he saw it—of established Christianity and against Hegel, felt compelled by his polemical situation to state his "point of view"; in like manner, today "everybody" seems to be for the formerly enslaved and colonized, and so it is necessary—for analogous reasons—to specify the "point of view," the stance, from which one writes. For a discussion of my conception of the "postcolonial sensibility," see E. C. Eze, "African Philosophy in Search of Identity: A Critical Response," *APA Newsletters* 95, no. 2 (spring 1996), p. 12.

25. Hannah Arendt, *Between Past and Future* (New York: Penguin Books, 1980), p. 6.

CHAPTER 1

1. Hasan Turabi, *Islam, Democracy, the State and the West* (a round table with Dr. Hasan Turabi, 10 May 1992), ed. Arthur L. Lowrie, transcribed by Maria Schone (World and Islam Studies Enterprise and the University of South Florida, Committee for Middle Eastern Studies), p. 13. To note this situation, as I have done, is to neither condone nor condemn Islamic fundamentalism but to recognize the cultural strength and vigor—held in reserve in most formerly colonized territories—that can be tapped or retrieved in ways that are destructive or fruitful, depending on the perspective that one takes, on the present and on the possibilities of a multicultural future for humanity. On this, see also Hussein Hijazi's interview of Mahmud Zahhar, spokesman of Hamas in Gaza/Palestine, "Hamas: Waiting for Secular Nationalism to Self-Destruct," *Journal of Palestine Studies* 24, no. 3 (spring 1995), pp. 81–88.

2. Kwame Nkrumah, *Consciencism* (New York: Monthly Review Press, 1970), chap. 3.

3. Paulin J. Hountondji, *African Philosophy, Myth and Reality*, 2nd edition (Bloomington: Indiana University Press, 1996), p. 53.

4. Ibid., chap. 4, parts 1 and 2.

5. On this, see Theophilus Okere, *African Philosophy: A Historico-Hermeneutical Investigation of the Conditions of Its Possibility* (Lanham, Md.: University Press of America, 1983), p. vii; Okonda W'oleko Okolo, *Pour une philosophie de la culture et du développement* (Kinshasa: Presses Universitaires du Zaire, 1986), p. 41.

6. Hans-Georg Gadamer, *Truth and Method* (New York: Crossroad Publishing Co., 1982), p. 268. The term *effective-history* is Gadamer's way of appropriating Martin Heidegger's view that the human *Dasein* projects a future out of its lived past or "has been"; that is, the future comes out of the past. The term thus describes and appropriates the historicity of human existence as established by Heidegger in *Being and Time*, trans. John Macquarrie and Ewared Robinson (New York: Harper & Row Publishers, 1962), see div. 2, sec. 69, passim, and specifically p. 416; sec. 68 and 73, passim, and specifically p. 430; and sec. 74, passim. On this point, see also Tsenay Serequeberhan, "Heidegger and Gadamer: Thinking as 'Meditative' and as 'Effective-Historical Consciousness,'" *Man and World* 20 (1987), pp. 41–64.

7. What I am proposing, then, is a rather limited reading of Fanon centered on the question of heritage. For more general contemporary explorations of Fanon, see *Fanon: A Critical Reader*, ed. Lewis R. Gordon, T. Denean Sharpley-Whiting, and Renée T. White (Cambridge, Mass.: Blackwell Publishers, 1996); Tsenay Serequeberhan, "Fanon and the Contemporary Discourse of African Philosophy," in *Fanon: A Critical Reader*, ed. Lewis R. Gordon, T. Denean Sharpley-Whiting, and Renée T. White (Cambridge, Mass.: Blackwell Publishers, 1996), pp. 244–55; T. Denean Sharpley-Whiting, *Frantz Fanon: Conflicts and Feminisms* (Lanham, Md.: Rowman & Littlefield Publishers, 1998); Ato Sekyi-Otu, *Fanon's Dialectic of Experience* (Cambridge, Mass.: Harvard University Press, 1996); and Lewis R. Gordon, *Fanon and the Crisis of European Man* (New York: Routledge, 1995).

8. Marcien Towa, "Propositions sur l'identité culturelle," *Présence Africaine* 109 (1st Quarter, 1979), p. 82, emphasis added.

9. On this point, see Lilyan Kesteloot, *Intellectual Origins of the African Revolu-*

tion (Washington, D.C.: Black Orpheus Press, 1972). Kesteloot focuses on francophone Africa, but, mutatis mutandis, all that she says is directly pertinent to the rest of the continent.

10. Cheikh Hamidou Kane, *L'Aventure ambiguë* (Paris: Julliard, 1961), p. 164; and *Ambiguous Adventure,* trans. Katherine Woods (Portsmouth, N.H.: Heinemann Educational Books Inc., 1989), p. 150.

11. Kane, *L'Aventure ambiguë,* p. 164; and *Ambiguous Adventure,* p. 151.

12. Frantz Fanon, *Peau noire masques blancs* (Paris: Éditions du Seuil, 1952), p. 8; and *Black Skin, White Masks,* trans. Charles Lam Markmann (New York: Grove Press Inc., 1967), p. 8. I have slightly altered the translation.

13. Ferdinand Oyono, *Houseboy* (Portsmouth, N.H.: Heinemann Educational Books Inc., 1990), p. 4.

14. Fanon, *Peau noire masques blancs,* p. 11; and *Black Skin, White Masks,* p. 12. I have slightly altered the translation.

15. Aimé Césaire, *Discours sur le colonialisme* (Paris and Dakar: Présence Africaine, 1955), p. 20; and *Discourse on Colonialism,* trans. Joan Pinkham (New York: Monthly Review Press, 1972), p. 22.

16. Amilcar Cabral, "National Liberation and Culture," in *Return to the Source: Selected Speeches* (New York: Monthly Review Press, 1973), p. 49.

17. This is what Fanon refers to as the "nationalist parties," in *The Wretched of the Earth,* trans. Constance Farrington (New York: Grove Press Inc., 1968).

18. Sembène Ousmane, *Xala* (Chicago: Lawrence Hill Books, 1976), p. 84.

19. On this, see Gadamer's remarks on Aristotle and the difference between "ethos" and *"physis,"* in *Truth and Method,* p. 279.

20. Frantz Fanon, *Les Damnés de la terre* (Paris: François Maspero, 1974), p. 14; and *The Wretched of the Earth,* p. 46.

21. Heidegger, *Being and Time,* p. 27.

22. Okere, *African Philosophy,* p. vii; Okolo, *Pour une philosophie de la culture et du développement,* p. 41; Towa, "Propositions sur l'identité culturelle," p. 82.

23. Fanon, *Les Damnés de la terre,* p. 145; and *The Wretched of the Earth,* p. 211.

24. Basil Davidson, *Africa in Modern History* (New York: Penguin Books, 1985), pp. 82–83.

25. Ibid., p. 43.

26. Towa, "Propositions sur l'identité culturelle," p. 82.

27. Fanon, *The Wretched of the Earth,* p. 209. I have slightly altered the translation.

28. Edward W. Said, *The Pen and the Sword* (Monroe, Maine: Common Courage Press, 1994), p. 66.

29. Jean-Paul Sartre, "Preface," in Frantz Fanon, *The Wretched of the Earth,* trans. Constance Farrington (New York: Grove Press Inc., 1968), p. 9.

30. Fanon, *Peau noire masques blancs,* p. 8; and *Black Skin, White Masks,* p. 8.

31. Said, *The Pen and the Sword,* p. 151.

32. On this, see Basil Davidson and Antonio Bronda, *Cross Roads in Africa* (Nottingham: Spokesman Publishing, Bertrand Russell House, 1980), p. 19.

33. Immanuel Wallerstein, *Historical Capitalism* (New York: Verso, 1987), p. 85.

34. Fanon, *Peau noire masques blancs,* p. 16; and *Black Skin, White Masks,* p. 18.

35. Fanon, *The Wretched of the Earth,* p. 222.

36. Franz Kafka, "In the Penal Colony," *Franz Kafka, Selected Short Stories,* ed. Philip Rahv (New York: The Modern Library, 1952), pp. 90–128.

37. Franz Kafka, "Report to an Academy," *Franz Kafka, Selected Short Stories* (New York: The Modern Library, 1952), p. 173.

38. Wole Soyinka, *Myth, Literature and the African World* (New York and Cambridge: Cambridge University Press, 1990), p. x.

39. W. E. B. Du Bois, *The Souls of Black Folk,* ed. David W. Blight and Robert Gooding-Williams (Boston and New York: Bedford Books, 1997), p. 233.

40. Kathleen Freeman, *Ancilla to the Pre-Socratic Philosophers* (Cambridge, Mass.: Harvard University Press, 1983), p. 32, fragment 119.

41. Sembène, *Xala,* p. 84.

42. Gadamer, *Truth and Method,* pp. 267–68.

43. Fanon, *Les Damnés de la terre,* p. 141; and *The Wretched of the Earth,* p. 206. I have slightly altered the translation.

44. Heidegger, *Being and Time,* pp. 319–25. See also Emmanuel Levinas, *Ethics and Infinity* (Pittsburgh: Duquesne University Press, 1985), pp. 95–101.

45. Emmanuel Levinas, *Existence and Existents* (The Hague: Martinus Nijhoff Publishing, 1978), p. 79.

46. Ibid., p. 99.

47. Tsenay Serequeberhan, *The Hermeneutics of African Philosophy* (New York: Routledge, 1994), p. 9.

48. This is the encounter and fusion of the horizons of the urban and rural native discussed in Serequeberhan, *The Hermeneutics of African Philosophy,* pp. 93–96. On this point, see also Tsenay Serequeberhan, "Africanity at the End of the 20th Century," *African Philosophy* 11, no. 1 (June 1998).

49. Césaire, *Discours sur le colonialisme,* p. 20; and *Discourse on Colonialism,* p. 22. Cabral, "National Liberation and Culture," p. 49.

50. Towa, "Propositions sur l'identité culturelle," p. 83.

51. Gadamer, *Truth and Method,* p. 269.

52. Ibid., p. 271.

53. Sartre, "Preface," p. 9.

54. Ibid., p. 11. This does not mean that Fanon was against socialism or that he did not value the "peasant class."

55. Fanon, *The Wretched of the Earth,* p. 106.

56. Sartre, "Preface," p. 10.

57. Frantz Fanon, *Sociologie d'une révolution* (Paris: François Maspero, 1978), pp. 136–54.

58. Albert Memmi, *The Colonizer and the Colonized* (Boston: Beacon Press, 1967), pp. 19–44.

59. Gadamer, *Truth and Method,* p. 266.

60. Ibid.

61. Ibid., pp. 264–65. This is the function of what Gadamer refers to as "temporal distance." In the present context, Heidegger's notion of "de-severance" (*Being and Time,* sec. 23, pp. 138–45) gives us a better sense of the developments being described.

62. On this, see Frantz Fanon, *Dying Colonialism* (New York: Monthly Review Press), appendixes 1 and 2, the testimonials of C. Geromini and B. Yvon, two *pied noir* who joined

the Algerian resistance. See also what Fanon says regarding "truth" in *Dying Colonialism,* p. 87; and *The Wretched of the Earth,* p. 50.

63. Albert Camus, *Neither Victims nor Executioners* (New York: Continuum Publishing Co., 1980).

64. Sartre, "Preface," p. 25.

65. Fanon, *Sociologie d'une révolution,* p. 138.

66. Fanon, *Les Damnés de la terre,* p. 62; and *The Wretched of the Earth,* p. 232. I have slightly altered the translation.

67. On this point, see, for example, Amilcar Cabral, "Anonymous Soldiers for the United Nations," in *Revolution in Guinea: Selected Texts* (New York: Monthly Review Press, 1969), pp. 50–52.

68. Kane, *Ambiguous Adventure,* p. 79–80.

69. Memmi, *The Colonizer and the Colonized,* p. 43. It should also be noted in passing that the "ex-'native'" in being such—by dint of his or her very formation—has a much more inclusive horizon than the European radical and/or the "colonizer who refuses." On this, please see Said's analogous remarks regarding Jerusalem in *The Pen and the Sword,* pp. 61–62.

70. Fanon, *Sociologie d'une révolution,* p. 174.

71. This is what Robert Bernasconi celebrates as Fanon's new humanism in "Casting the Slough: Fanon's New Humanism for a New Humanity," in *Fanon: A Critical Reader,* ed. Lewis R. Gordon (Oxford and Cambridge: Blackwell Publishers, 1996), pp. 113–21.

72. Ibid., p. 121.

73. Fanon, *Sociologie d'une révolution,* p. 15.

74. Fanon, *The Wretched of the Earth,* p. 146. I have slightly altered the translation.

75. Ibid., pp. 145–46; and *Les Damnés de la terre,* pp. 92–93.

76. Césaire, *Discours sur le colonialisme,* p. 20; and *Discourse on Colonialism,* p. 22. Cabral, "National Liberation and Culture," p. 49. Towa, "Propositions sur l'identité culturelle," p. 83.

77. Fanon, *The Wretched of the Earth,* pp. 315–16; and *Les Damnés de la terre,* pp. 232–33. I have slightly altered the translation.

78. Fanon, *The Wretched of the Earth,* p. 246; and *Les Damnés de la terre,* p. 144.

79. Gadamer, *Truth and Method,* p. 250.

80. Fanon, *Les Damnés de la terre,* p. 173.

81. Martin Heidegger, "Letter on Humanism," in *Martin Heidegger, Basic Writings,* ed. D. F. Krell (New York: Harper & Row Publishers, 1977), p. 200. On this, see also Jacques Rabemananjara, "Europe and Ourselves," *Présence Africaine* 8–10 (June–November 1956), p. 21.

82. Heidegger, "Letter on Humanism," p. 202.

CHAPTER 2

1. Kwame Anthony Appiah, *In My Father's House* (New York: Oxford University Press, 1992), p. 30, emphasis added.

2. I have in mind three texts: Lucius Outlaw, "'Conserve' Races?" in *W. E. B. Du Bois on Race and Culture,* ed. B. W. Bell, E. R. Grosholz, and J. B. Stewart (New York: Rout-

ledge, 1996), pp. 15–37; Robert Gooding-Williams, "Outlaw, Appiah, and Du Bois's 'The Conservation of Races,'" in *W. E. B. Du Bois on Race and Culture,* ed. B. W. Bell, E. R. Grosholz, and J. B. Stewart (New York: Routledge, 1996) pp. 39–56; and Tommy Lot, "Du Bois on the Invention of Race," in *African-American Perspectives and Philosophical Traditions,* ed. J. P. Pittman (New York: Routledge, 1997), pp. 166–87.

3. I borrow this phrase from the title of Lewis R. Gordon's anthology, *Existence in Black* (New York: Routledge, 1997).

4. W. E. B. Du Bois, "The Conservation of Races," in part 2 of *The Souls of Black Folk,* ed. and introduced by David W. Blight and Robert Gooding-Williams (Boston: Bedford Books, 1997), p. 230.

5. Ibid., p. 228.

6. Ibid., p. 234.

7. Ibid., p. 235, emphasis added.

8. Ibid., p. 234.

9. Ibid., p. 233.

10. Ibid., p. 235.

11. Ibid., p. 236.

12. Ibid., p. 235.

13. Ibid., p. 237, emphasis added.

14. Ibid., p. 228.

15. This is what Appiah refers to as "the acceptance of difference" in *In My Father's House,* p. 30.

16. Du Bois, "The Conservation of Races," p. 237.

17. Léopold Sedar Senghor, quoted in Frantz Fanon, *Black Skin, White Masks,* trans. Charles Lam Markmann (New York: Grove Press, 1967), p. 127.

18. Du Bois, "The Conservation of Races," p. 229.

19. René Depestre, "An Interview with Aimé Césaire," in *Discourse on Colonialism,* ed. René Depestre (New York: Monthly Review Press, 1972), p. 76.

20. Du Bois, "The Conservation of Races," p. 230.

21. Hans-Georg Gadamer, *Truth and Method* (New York: Crossroad Publishing Co., 1982), p. 15.

22. Ibid., p. 12.

23. Ibid.

24. Du Bois, "The Conservation of Races," p. 233.

25. Appiah, *In My Father's House,* p. 30.

26. Emmanuel Levinas, quoted in Robert Bernasconi, "Who Is My Neighbor? Who Is the Other? Questioning 'the Generosity of Western Thought,'" in *Ethics and Responsibility in the Phenomenological Tradition* (Pittsburgh: Duquesne University Press, 1992), p. 9.

27. Appiah, *In My Father's House,* p. 30.

28. Jean-Paul Sartre, *Black Orpheus* (Paris: Présence Africaine, 1976), p. 59. For an insightful critique of this text, see Lewis R. Gordon, *Bad Faith and Antiblack Racism* (Atlantic Highlands, N.J.: Humanities Press, 1995), p. 4.

29. Levinas, in Bernasconi, "Who Is My Neighbor? Who Is the Other?" p. 9.

30. Martin Heidegger, *Being and Time,* trans. John Macquarrie and Eward Robinson (New York: Harper & Row Publishers, 1962), p. 83.

31. This is what Aimé Césaire refers to as "chosification" in *Discours sur le colonialisme* (Paris and Dakar: Présence Africaine, 1955), p. 19.

32. Fanon, *Black Skin, White Masks*, p. 14; and *Peau noire masques blancs* (Paris: Éditions du Seuil, 1952), p. 13. I have slightly altered the translation.

33. Fanon, *Black Skin, White Masks*, p. 140; and *Peau noire masques blancs*, pp. 115–16.

34. Fanon, *Black Skin, White Masks*, chap. 5, passim. The title of this chapter, which the introduction states "is important for more than one reason," is rendered in the standard translation as "The Fact of Blackness." A more accurate translation of "L 'Expérience vécue du Noir" would be "The Lived Experience of the Black."

35. Sartre, *Black Orpheus*, p. 41.

36. Ibid., pp. 60–61.

37. Fanon, *Black Skin, White Masks*, p. 138; and *Peau noire masques blancs*, p. 114.

38. Fanon, *Black Skin, White Masks*, p. 221.

39. Edward W. Said, "Yeats and Decolonization," in *Nationalism, Colonialism and Literature*, ed. and introduction by Seamus Deane (Minneapolis: University of Minnesota Press, 1990), p. 82.

40. Du Bois, "The Conservation of Races," p. 233.

41. Heidegger, *Being and Time*, p. 67.

42. Martin Luther King Jr., *I Have a Dream: Writings and Speeches That Changed the World*, ed. J. M. Washington (San Francisco: HarperCollins Publishers, 1992), p. 6.

43. Booker T. Washington, *Up from Slavery*, ed. Philip Smith (New York: Dover Publications Inc., 1995), pp. 11–12.

44. Gadamer, *Truth and Method*, p. 15.

45. Frantz Fanon, *The Wretched of the Earth*, trans. Constance Farrington (New York: Grove Press Inc., 1968), p. 36; and *Les Damnés de la terre* (Paris: François Maspero, 1974), p. 6.

46. Rosa Parks, quoted in King, *I Have a Dream*, p. 5.

47. Malcolm X, *The Final Speeches*, ed. Steve Clark (New York: Pathfinder, 1992), p. 265.

48. Ibid., p. 266.

49. Du Bois, "The Conservation of Races," p. 233.

50. James H. Cone, *Martin & Malcolm & America: A Dream or a Nightmare* (New York: Orbis Books, 1995), p. x.

51. Depestre, "An Interview with Aimé Césaire," p. 76.

52. W. E. B. Du Bois, *The Souls of Black Folk*, ed. and introduced by David W. Blight and Robert Gooding-Williams (Boston: Bedford Books, 1997), p. 39.

53. Ibid., pp. 38, 163.

54. Ibid., p. 158.

CHAPTER 3

1. *The History of Mary Prince a West Indian Slave Related by Herself*, ed. and introduced by Moira Ferguson (Ann Arbor: University of Michigan Press, 1987), p. 17.

2. Ibid., p. 35, note 31.

3. Alexandre Kojève, *Introduction to the Reading of Hegel: Lectures on the Phenomenology of Spirit,* assembled by Raymond Queneau, ed. Allan Bloom, trans. James H. Nichols Jr. (Ithaca and London: Cornell University Press, 1993), p. 30.

4. On this point, see Frantz Fanon, *Black Skin, White Masks,* trans. Charles Lam Markmann (New York: Grove Press, 1967), chap. 7, sec. B, "The Negro and Hegel," pp. 216–22.

5. *Hegel's Phenomenology of Spirit,* trans. A. V. Miller, with analysis and foreword by J. N. Findley (New York and Oxford: Oxford University Press, 1977), p. 56.

6. Joseph L. Navickas, *Consciousness and Reality: Hegel's Philosophy of Subjectivity* (The Hague: Martinus Nijhoff, 1976), p. 3.

7. *Hegel's Phenomenology of Spirit,* p. 103, paragraph 165.

8. Ibid., p. 104, paragraph 166.

9. Ibid., p. 111, paragraph 178.

10. Ibid., p. 110, paragraph 175.

11. *Hegel's Science of Logic,* trans. A. V. Miller (New York: Humanities Press, 1976), p. 53.

12. Ibid.

13. Ibid., p. 54.

14. Ibid.

15. Hans-Georg Gadamer, *Hegel's Dialectic* (New Haven: Yale University Press, 1976), p. 83.

16. Jean Hypolite, *Studies on Marx and Hegel* (New York: Harper & Row Publishers, 1969), p. 9.

17. *Hegel's Science of Logic,* p. 54.

18. Ibid., p. 55.

19. Ibid., p. 442.

20. Hans-Georg Gadamer, *Truth and Method* (New York: Crossroad Publishing Co., 1982), pp. 310–11.

21. On this, see Henry Louis Gates Jr., "Introduction," in *The Classical Slave Narratives,* ed. Henry Louis Gates Jr. (New York: A Mentor Book, 1987), pp. ix–xviii.

22. Frederick Douglass, *Narrative of the Life of Frederick Douglass an American Slave Written by Himself* (New York: A Signet Book, 1968), p. 77.

23. Ibid., p. 26.

24. Ibid., p. 22.

25. Ibid., p. 83.

26. Ibid., p. 25.

27. Ibid., p. 23.

28. Ibid., p. 29. See also Ferguson, *The History of Mary Prince,* p. 53, footnote.

29. Douglass, *Narrative of the Life of Frederick Douglass,* p. 31.

30. Ibid., p. 36.

31. Ibid., p. 37.

32. Ibid., p. 31.

33. Ibid., pp. 39–40.

34. *Hegel's Phenomenology of Spirit,* pp. 114–15, paragraph 188.

35. Douglass, *Narrative of the Life of Frederick Douglass,* p. 83.

36. *Hegel's Phenomenology of Spirit,* p. 114, paragraph 187.

37. Ferguson, *The History of Mary Prince,* p. 64, emphasis added.

38. Douglass, *Narrative of the Life of Frederick Douglass,* chap. 8.

39. *Hegel's Phenomenology of Spirit,* p. 114, paragraph 187.

40. Douglass, *Narrative of the Life of Frederick Douglass,* p. 83.

41. Ibid., pp. 81–82.

42. At this point I depart from a strict exposition of Hegel's master-slave dialectic, for my sole concern is to show how the freedom of recognition is secured by the formerly enslaved.

43. Douglass, *Narrative of the Life of Frederick Douglass,* p. 82.

44. Frantz Fanon, *Black Skin, White Masks,* trans. Charles Lam Markmann (New York: Grove Press, 1967), p. 221.

45. For a different and in my view not very fruitful way of reading Hegel, see Cynthia Willet, "The Master-Slave Dialectic: Hegel vs. Douglass," in *Subjugation & Bondage,* ed. Tommy L. Lott (Lanham, Md.: Rowman & Littlefield Publishers Inc., 1998), pp. 151–70.

46. Maya Angelou, "Still I Rise," in *Phenomenal Woman* (New York: Random House Publishers, 1994), p. 9.

CHAPTER 4

1. *Proceedings and Addresses of the American Philosophical Association* 68, no. 4 (February 1995), p. 30.

2. *Proceedings and Addresses of the American Philosophical Association* 27, no. 1 (Spring 1996), pp. 110–18.

3. *Plato's Republic,* trans. G. M. A. Grube (Indianapolis: Hackett Publishing Co., 1974), p. 4, #329d.

4. Ibid., p. 25, #352d.

5. For the record I would like to note that I do not descend from kings or emperors. I am an Eritrean who grew up in Ethiopia because both my paternal and maternal grandfathers—ordinary Africans—had to flee Italian Eritrea after having had violent confrontations with the Italian colonial authorities of the time.

6. Tsenay Serequeberhan, *The Hermeneutics of African Philosophy* (New York: Routledge, 1994).

7. The conclusion of the Eritrean war of independence in May 1991 and the independence referendum of April 1993 were events carried out with a great deal of civility and diplomatic astuteness on both sides. In spite of the recent border dispute between Eritrea and Ethiopia (which started in July 1997 and erupted into open conflict in May 1998), these political eventuations of the early 1990s have to be seen as triumphs for African politics and diplomacy.

8. For an interesting assessment of this situation, which already seems to have been overtaken by events, see Philip Gourevitch, "Continental Shift," *The New Yorker,* 4 August 1997, pp. 42–55.

9. This is the general sense that I get from Appiah's overall stance.

10. Kwame Anthony Appiah, *In My Father's House* (New York and Oxford: Oxford University Press, 1992), p. 98.

11. Ibid.

12. On this point, see P. O. Bodunrin's critique of Oruka in "Which Kind of Philosophy for Africa," in *Philosophy in the Present Situation of Africa,* ed. Alwin Diemer (Wiesbaden: Steiner, 1981), pp. 8–22. For an interesting recent discussion of Oruka's project, see Bruce Janz, "Thinking Wisdom: The Hermeneutical Basis of Sage Philosophy," *African Philosophy* 11, no. 1 (June 1998): 57–71.

13. Appiah, *In My Father's House,* p. 106.

14. Ibid., p. 95.

15. Marcien Towa, "Conditions for the Affirmation of a Modern African Philosophical Thought," in *African Philosophy: The Essential Readings,* ed. Tsenay Serequeberhan (New York: Paragon House, 1991), p. 191.

16. Ibid., p. 196.

17. Ibid., p. 194.

18. Appiah, *In My Father's House,* p. 98.

19. Ibid., p. 106.

20. I recently had a nice conversation with Hountondji at the Twentieth World Congress of Philosophy in Boston, and, even though I have not seen anything in print yet, he reassured me that in his new book—published by a local publisher in Benin and not yet available to the Diaspora community—his views have changed substantially.

21. For Marcien Towa's systematic articulation of this perspective, see *Essai sur la problématique philosophique dans l'Afrique actuelle* (Yaoundé: Editions Clé, 1971).

22. Appiah, *In My Father's House,* p. 120.

23. Ibid., p. 135.

24. Ibid., p. 129.

25. Ibid., p. 127.

26. Ibid., p. 129.

27. Ibid.

28. Ibid., p. 130.

29. Ibid., p. 131.

30. The following quotation, also noted above, can only mean that Africans are naturally predisposed to believe in multiple spiritual forces: "It is this belief in the plurality of invisible spiritual forces that makes possible the—to Western eyes—extraordinary spectacle of a Catholic bishop praying at a Methodist wedding in tandem with traditional royal appeal to the ancestors" (Appiah, *In My Father's House,* p. 135).

31. Sembène Ousmane, *Xala* (Chicago: Lawrence Hill Books, 1976), pp. 3–4.

32. Marcien Towa, "Propositions sur l'identité culturelle," *Présence Africaine* 109 (1st Quarter, 1979).

33. Frantz Fanon, *Les Damnés de la terre* (Paris: François Maspero, 1974), pp. 229–33. Amilcar Cabral, "Identity and Dignity in the Context of the National Liberation Struggle," in *Return to the Source: Selected Speeches* (New York: Monthly Review Press, 1973), p. 63.

34. Appiah, *In My Father's House,* p. 170.

35. Ibid., p. 157.

36. Towa, "Propositions sur l'identité culturelle," p. 85.

37. Chinua Achebe, *Anthills of the Savannah* (New York: Anchor Books, 1989), p. 210.

38. Cabral, "Identity and Dignity in the Context of the National Liberation Struggle," p. 63. See also Amilcar Cabral, "The Weapon of Theory," in *Revolution in Guinea: Selected*

Texts (New York: Monthly Review Press, 1969), passim. For a detailed discussion of Cabral on this point, see the last chapter of Serequeberhan, *The Hermeneutics of African Philosophy.*

39. Appiah, *In My Father's House,* p. 155.

40. Dan Connell, *Against All Odds: A Chronicle of the Eritrean Revolution* (Trenton: The Red Sea Press, 1993).

41. Towa, "Propositions sur l'identité culturelle," passim.

42. Sembène Ousmane, *The Last of the Empire* (London, Ibadan, and Nairobi: Heinemann Educational Books Ltd., 1983), p. 135.

43. Appiah, *In My Father's House,* pp. 81–82.

44. Ibid., p. 176.

45. Ibid., p. 81.

46. Note in this regard Fanon's critical remarks on Sartre's *Black Orpheus* in *Black Skins, White Masks,* trans. Charles Lam Markmann (New York: Grove Press Inc., 1967), pp. 132–40.

47. In this regard, see President Isayas Afwerki, "Opening Address to the Organization of African Unity Heads of State Summit," presented in Cairo, Egypt, 28 June 1993, in *Eritrea Update,* July 1993.

48. Appiah, *In My Father's House,* p. 180.

49. Ibid., p. 177.

50. Ibid., p. 180.

51. Ibid., p. 177.

52. Ibid.

53. Achebe, *Anthills of the Savannah,* p. 114, emphasis added.

54. Afwerki, "Opening Address," p. 2.

55. Hans-Georg Gadamer, *Truth and Method* (New York: Crossroad Publishing Co., 1982), p. 245.

56. Afwerki, "Opening Address," p. 2.

57. Ernest Wamba-dia-Wamba, "Philosophy in Africa: Challenges of the African Philosopher," in *African Philosophy: The Essential Readings,* ed. Tsenay Serequeberhan (New York: Paragon House, 1991).

58. Theophilus Okere, *African Philosophy: A Historico-Hermeneutical Investigation of the Conditions of Its Possibility* (Lanham, Md.: University Press of America, 1983), p. v. By the term *postcolonial* I mean the contradictory situation left by colonialism and the concrete political struggles and contradictions through which the formerly colonized (i.e., the peoples of the Third World) have constituted themselves as "independent" nation-states. For an interesting critique of the variegated uses this term has been put to, please see Aijaz Ahmad, "The Politics of Literary Postcoloniality," in *Race & Class* 36, no. 3 (January–March 1995).

59. Aimé Césaire, *Discourse on Colonialism,* trans. Joan Pinkham (New York: Monthly Review Press, 1972), p. 76.

60. Patrice Lumumba, *Lumumba Speaks* (Boston and Toronto: Little, Brown & Co., 1972), p. 429.

61. In this regard, Immanuel Kant refers to the inhabitants of Tahiti—and by extension non-Europeans as such—as being no better than "sheep and cattle," in "Reviews of Herder's Ideas for a Philosophy of the History of Mankind," in *Kant on History,* ed. Lewis White Beck (Indianapolis: Bobbs-Merrill Co., Inc., 1963), p. 51.

62. Cabral, "The Weapon of Theory," p. 52.

63. Okonda Okolo, "Tradition and Destiny: Horizons of an African Philosophical Hermeneutics," in *African Philosophy: The Essential Readings,* ed. Tsenay Serequeberhan (New York: Paragon House, 1991), p. 207.

64. Aimé Césaire, *Lettre à Maurice Thorez* (Paris: Présence Africaine, 1956), p. 8.

65. On this point, please see Césaire, *Lettre à Maurice Thorez,* and the talk given by President Isayas Afwerki, "Achieving Global Human Security: Eritrea's View," presented at the International Development Conference in Washington, D.C., 16–18 January 1995, in *Eritrea Profile* 1, no. 45 (11 February 1995). See also Afwerki's statement to the forty-eighth session of the United Nations General Assembly, New York, 30 September 1993.

CHAPTER 5

1. Benjamin E. Oguah, "African and Western Philosophy: A Comparative Study," in *African Philosophy,* ed. Richard Wright (Lanham, Md.: University Press of America, 1984), p. 213.

2. E. C. Eze, ed., *Postcolonial African Philosophy* (Cambridge, Mass.: Blackwell Publishers, 1997), p. 2.

3. A good example of this is David Stewart and H. Gene Blocker, *Fundamentals of Philosophy* (Upper Saddle River, N.J.: Prentice Hall, 1996). That this text does not contain a section on African philosophy is surprising because Blocker has been teaching for many years in Nigeria and has himself dabbled, a bit, in African philosophy.

4. Robert C. Solomon and Kathleen M. Higgins, *A Short History of Philosophy* (New York and Oxford: Oxford University Press, 1996), pp. 292–99.

5. David E. Cooper, *World Philosophies: An Historical Introduction* (Oxford and Cambridge: Blackwell Publishers, 1996), pp. 396–408.

6. Martin Heidegger, *What Is Philosophy?* (New Haven: College and University Press Publishers, 1956), p. 31.

7. Cornelius Castoriadis, "Intellectuals and History," in *Philosophy, Politics, Autonomy,* ed. David Ames Curtis (New York and Oxford: Oxford University Press, 1991), p. 4.

8. Marcien Towa, "Conditions for the Affirmation of a Modern African Philosophical Thought," in *African Philosophy: The Essential Readings,* ed. Tsenay Serequeberhan (New York: Paragon House, 1991), p. 194.

9. It is necessary to proceed along this very unusual way precisely because in more cases than not this unexamined prejudice is not viewed as such in most contemporary Euro-American philosophical circles.

10. *African Philosophy/La Philosophie Africaine,* ed. Claude Sumner (Addis Ababa: Chamber Printing House for Addis Ababa University, 1980), p. xv.

11. Claude Sumner, "Ethiopia: Land of Diverse Expressions of Philosophy, Birthplace of Modern Thought," in *African Philosophy/La Philosophie Africaine,* ed. Claude Sumner (Addis Ababa: Chamber Printing House for Addis Ababa University, 1980), pp. 392–400.

12. I say *Abyssinian* and not *Ethiopian* because, as Sumner points out, this is the proper designation of the area in question. See Claude Sumner, ed., *Classical Ethiopian Philosophy* (Addis Ababa: Commercial Printing Press, 1985), p. 1.

13. Marcien Towa, *L'Idée d'une philosophie négro-africaine* (Yaoundé: Editions Clé, 1979), p. 5.

14. Romano Guardini, *The End of the Modern World* (Chicago: Henry Regenery Co., 1968), p. 45.

15. Hans-Georg Gadamer, *Reason in the Age of Science* (Cambridge, Mass.: MIT Press, 1981), p. 6.

16. Immanuel Kant, *Critique of Pure Reason*, trans. Norman Kemp Smith (New York: St. Martin's Press, 1965), p. 29.

17. Joseph Pieper, *Scholasticism* (New York: McGraw-Hill, 1964), pp. 150–51. Interestingly enough, three centuries after the fact, Pope John Paul II is presently calling for the reunification of faith and reason (Alessander Stanley, "Pope Calls on the World to Reunite Faith and Reason," *New York Times,* 16 October 1998, front page).

18. For this notion of philosophy as a critical-cultural inventory, please see Antonio Gramsci, *Quaderni del carcere,* vol. 2, *Edizione critica dell'Istituto Gramsci, a cura di Valentino Gerratana* (Torino, Italy: Giulio Einaudi, 1975), p. 1376.

19. On this point regarding Western philosophy, see also Lansana Keita, "Contemporary African Philosophy: The Search for a Method," in *African Philosophy: The Essential Readings,* ed. Tsenay Serequeberhan (New York: Paragon House, 1991), pp. 144–45.

20. Kant, *Critique of Pure Reason,* p. 20.

21. Towa, "Conditions for the Affirmation of a Modern African Philosophical Thought," p. 194.

22. Towa, *L'Idée d'une philosophie négro-africaine,* p. 7, emphasis added.

23. I will only present a limited discussion of the first of these two thinkers, for I am not concerned with their thinking, as such, but with a concise illustration of its philosophic nature.

24. *Classical Ethiopian Philosophy,* ed. Claude Sumner (Addis Ababa: Addis Ababa University/Commercial Printing Press, 1985), p. 235.

25. Gadamer, *Reason in the Age of Science,* p. 6.

26. Quoted in *Classical Ethiopian Philosophy,* ed. Claude Sumner, p. 235. In my native Tigringia, a language rooted in Ge'ez, the word for question is *hito,* and the term *hatäta* signifies a process of generalized questioning.

27. Castoriadis, "Intellectuals and History," p. 4.

28. Kant, *Critique of Pure Reason,* p. 20.

29. Ibid., p. 29.

30. Towa, "Conditions for the Affirmation of a Modern African Philosophical Thought," p. 194.

31. Ibid., pp. 194–95.

32. *Hegel's Philosophy of Right,* trans. T. M. Knox (New York and Oxford: Oxford University Press, 1976), p. 11.

33. Towa, *L'Idée d'une philosophie négro-africaine,* pp. 33, 36.

34. Ibid., p. 32.

35. Ibid., pp. 32, 34–35.

36. Ibid., pp. 40–41, 44.

37. Ibid., pp. 42–43, 46–47.

38. Romano Guardini, *The Death of Socrates* (Cleveland and New York: Meridian Books, 1965), p. 6.

39. Ibid., pp. 38, 41.

40. Ibid., pp. 71, 79, emphasis added.

41. On this point, see Tsenay Serequeberhan, "Eurocentrism in Philosophy: The Case of Immanuel Kant," *The Philosophical Forum* 27, no. 4 (summer 1996), pp. 333–56.

42. Friedrich Nietzsche, *The Gay Science* (New York: Vintage Books, 1974), no. 108, p. 167.

43. Ibid., no. 343, p. 279.

44. Paulin J. Hountondji, "Scientific Dependence in Africa Today," *Research in African Literatures* 21, no. 3 (fall 1990), p. 7, emphasis added.

45. Ibid.

46. Ibid., p. 6.

47. Ibid.

48. Ibid., p. 7.

49. Immanuel Wallerstein, *Historical Capitalism* (New York: Verso Press, 1987), p. 80.

50. Ibid., p. 81.

51. Ibid., p. 80.

52. Ibid., p. 81.

53. Ibid., p. 83.

54. Ibid.

55. Ibid.

56. Ibid., p. 82.

57. On this point, see Tsenay Serequeberhan, *The Hermeneutics of African Philosophy* (New York: Routledge, 1994), pp. 33–42.

58. Frantz Fanon, *Peau noire masques blancs* (Paris: Éditions du Seuil, 1952), p. 31.

59. On this, see also Serequeberhan, *The Hermeneutics of African Philosophy,* p. 40.

60. Cornelius Castoriadis, "Reflections on 'Rationality' and 'Development': Presentation and Response to Critics," in *Philosophy, Politics, Autonomy,* ed. David Ames Curtis (New York and Oxford: Oxford University Press, 1991), p. 198.

61. Ibid., pp. 200–201.

62. Jose Rabasa, *Inventing America* (Norman and London: University of Oklahoma Press, 1993), p. 18.

63. To my knowledge, Hountondji's latest published remarks on this point, "Producing Knowledge in Africa Today" (*African Studies Review* 38, no. 3 [December 1995]), a follow-up to his 1990 article, do not add substantially to the position articulated in the previous paper.

64. Martin Heidegger, *Being and Time,* trans. John Macquarrie and Ewared Robinson (New York: Harper & Row Publishers, 1962), p. 437.

65. Amilcar Cabral, *Return to the Source: Selected Speeches* (New York: Monthly Review Press, 1973), p. 63.

66. I first show this connection in the thinking of Cabral and Heidegger in *The Hermeneutics of African Philosophy,* pp. 126–27, note 16; and pp. 102–7. See also, on this point, Fred Dallmayr, *Alternative Visions* (Lanham, Md.: Rowman & Littlefield Publishers, Inc., 1998), pp. 169–90; and Robert Bernasconi, "African Philosophy's Challenge to Continental Philosophy," in *Postcolonial African Philosophy,* ed. E. C. Eze (Cambridge, Mass.: Blackwell Publishers, 1997), p. 189.

67. Amilcar Cabral, "National Liberation and Culture," in *Return to the Source: Selected Speeches* (New York: Monthly Review Press, 1973), p. 52, emphasis added.

68. Ibid., p. 53.

69. Theophilus Okere, "The Relation between Culture and Philosophy," *Journal of the Department of Philosophy, University of Nigeria, Nsukka* 2 (1976), pp. 9–11.

70. Nietzsche, *The Gay Science*, no. 108, p. 167.

71. In the first section of this chapter, I do engage in precisely what I am criticizing at this point. But this was necessary—not so much to show that we had philosophy and philosophers in the African past but to concretely rebut the prejudice against African philosophy that still endures among Euro-American philosophers.

72. This fusion, furthermore, has to be undertaken in full awareness—and in critical rejection—of the malignant hubris that has been, and is still, the driving force of science and technology as produced out of the historicity of European modernity.

73. Frantz Fanon, *Les Damnés de la terre* (Paris: François Maspero, 1974), p. 162; and *The Wretched of the Earth*, trans. Constance Farrington (New York: Grove Press Inc., 1968), p. 232.

74. Friedrich Nietzsche, *On the Advantage and Disadvantage of History for Life*, trans. and introduction by Peter Preuss (Indianapolis: Hackett Publishing, 1986).

75. Marcien Towa, "Propositions sur l'identité culturelle," *Présence Africaine* 109 (1st Quarter, 1979), p. 90.

76. Okonda w'oleko Okolo, *Pour une philosophie de la culture et du développement* (Kinshasa: Presses Universitaires du Zaire, 1986), pp. 41–46.

77. Towa, "Propositions sur l'identité culturelle," p. 87.

78. Karl Marx, *Capital*, vol. 1, trans. S. Moore and E. Aveling, ed. Frederick Engels (New York: International Publishers, 1975), p. 751.

79. Basil Davidson, *Cross Roads in Africa* (Nottingham: Spokesman Press, 1980), p. 47.

80. Hountondji, "Scientific Dependence in Africa Today," p. 7.

81. Towa, "Propositions sur l'identité culturelle," p. 6.

82. R. J. Goldstein, "Preface," in Michel Foucault, *Remarks on Marx* (New York: Semiotext[e]), p. 9.

83. Towa, "Propositions sur l'identité culturelle," p. 6.

84. Marx, *Capital*, pp. 765, 713–74.

85. Hountondji, "Scientific Dependence in Africa Today," p. 7.

86. Towa, "Propositions sur l'identité culturelle," p. 10.

87. Robert Bernasconi, "Can Development Theory Break with Its Past? Endogenous Development in Africa and the Old Imperialism," *African Philosophy* 11, no. 1 (June 1998), pp. 23–34. See also Eiman O. Zein-Elabdin, "The Question of Development in Africa: A Conversation for Propitious Change," *African Philosophy* 11, no. 2 (November 1998), pp. 113–25.

88. Bernasconi, "Can Development Theory Break with Its Past?" p. 31.

89. Ibid. Bernasconi refers to this as the "European perspective."

90. Ibid.

91. On a specific elaboration of this critical point, see Isayas Afwerki's interview in J. Firebrace and S. Holland, *Never Kneel Down Eritrea* (Trenton: The Red Sea Press, 1986), pp. 127–40.

92. Chinua Achebe, *The Trouble with Nigeria* (Enugu, Nigeria: Fourth Dimension Publishers, 1983), p. 19.

93. Fanon, *Les Damnés de la terre*, p. 233.

CHAPTER 6

1. Edward W. Said, *The Pen and the Sword* (Monroe, Maine: Common Courage Press, 1994), p. 78.

2. Edward W. Said, *The Question of Palestine* (New York: Vintage Books, 1980), p. 77, emphasis added.

3. Placide Temples, *Bantu Philosophy* (Paris: Présence Africaine, 1969), p. 84.

4. For Kant and Hegel, as is well known, the Idée is the theoretic frame that guides thinking in both its speculative and practical undertakings. This is also true for Marx, even though he substitutes "material conditions" for the Idée.

5. On this point, see, for example, David Ingram, *Critical Theory and Philosophy* (New York: Paragon House Publishers, 1990), p. xv.

6. My concern is to show that these thinkers, in their historical thinking, buttress and give credence to the prejudice—the superiority complex—that to this day sanctions Western global domination. That they did not share our prejudices and concerns is to be expected. What needs exhibiting is how their philosophic thinking—in the name of human freedom—surreptitiously justifies Western dominance. In this regard, see also Tsenay Serequeberhan, "Eurocentrism in Philosophy: The Case of Immanuel Kant," *The Philosophical Forum* 27, no. 4 (summer 1996); "Karl Marx and African Emancipatory Thought: A Critique of Marx's Euro-Centric Metaphysics," *Praxis International* 10, nos. 1–2 (April and July 1990); and "The Idea of Colonialism in Hegel's *Philosophy of Right*," *International Philosophical Quarterly* 29, no. 3, issue 115 (September 1989).

7. Said, *The Pen and the Sword*, p. 78.

8. Adriaan Theodoor Peperzak, *Platonic Transformations* (Lanham, Md.: Rowman & Littlefield Publishers, Inc., 1997), p. ix.

9. Plato, *The Collected Dialogues* (Princeton: Princeton University Press, 1989), p. 1576, #326b.

10. Hannah Arendt, *Between Past and Future* (New York: Penguin Books, 1980), p. 11.

11. H. D. F. Kitto, *The Greeks* (Harmondsworth, U.K.: Penguin Books, 1979), pp. 7–11.

12. Plato, *The Collected Dialogues*, p. 710, #470e–471c.

13. Ibid., p. 712, #473b. (G. M. A. Grube prefers "theory" to "words.")

14. Ibid., pp. 707–11, #469b–471c.

15. Ibid., p. 710, #471b–c.

16. Ibid., p. 708, #469c.

17. Ibid.

18. Ibid., p. 710, #470d–e.

19. Ibid., p. 710, #470e. "America, love it or leave it" is the appropriate colloquial expression of the position Plato is articulating. In other words, ". . . , love it or leave it," filling the blank with the name of any Euro-American country, expresses quite well the generalized xenophobia that, from time to time, categorically defines Europe's relation with the rest of us.

20. Ibid., p. 709, #470c.

21. G. M. A. Grube, *Plato's Republic* (Indianapolis: Hackett Publishing Co., 1974), p. 130, #470c.

22. Ingram, *Critical Theory and Philosophy*, p. xv.

23. What I have labeled "false double negation" is similar to what Gianni Vattimo refers

to as "*la fallacia platonica*" in *Al di là del Soggetto* (Milan: Idee/Feltrinelli, 1984), pp. 12–13.

24. Notice that this does not apply to the Sophists who did not believe in slaves by nature; in fact, they are the ones against whom the tradition was established. On the other hand, Aristotle does not say much that is different from Plato in this regard.

25. Michel Foucault, "What Is Enlightenment?" in *Foucault Reader*, ed. Paul Rabinow (New York: Pantheon Books, 1984), p. 35.

26. Immanuel Kant, "An Old Question Raised Again: Is the Human Race Constantly Progressing?" in *Kant on History*, ed. Lewis White Beck (Indianapolis: Bobbs-Merrill Publishers, 1963), p. 137.

27. Foucault, "What Is Enlightenment?" p. 47.

28. Cornelius Castoriadis, "The Greek Polis and the Creation of Democracy," in *Philosophy, Politics, Autonomy*, ed. David Ames Curtis (New York and Oxford: Oxford University Press, 1991), p. 100.

29. Immanuel Kant, "Perpetual Peace," in *Kant on History*, ed. Lewis White Beck (Indianapolis: Bobbs-Merrill Publishers, 1963), p. 103.

30. Immanuel Kant, "Reviews of Herder's Ideas for a Philosophy of the History of Mankind," in *Kant on History*, ed. Lewis White Beck (Indianapolis: Bobbs-Merrill Publishers, 1963), pp. 50–51.

31. Ibid., p. 50.

32. Plato, *The Collected Dialogues*, p. 708, #469c.

33. Immanuel Kant, "Conjectural Beginning of Human History," in *Kant on History*, ed. Lewis White Beck (Indianapolis: Bobbs-Merrill Publishers, 1963), p. 58.

34. Ibid.

35. Ibid., pp. 59–60.

36. Kant, "Perpetual Peace," p. 98.

37. On Kant's disparaging opinion of non-Europeans as a whole, please see Immanuel Kant, *Observations on the Feeling of the Beautiful and Sublime*, ed. and trans. John T. Goldthwait (Berkeley, Los Angeles, and Oxford: University of California Press, 1991), pp. 97–116.

38. Plato, *The Collected Dialogues*, p. 708, #469c.

39. Immanuel Kant, "Idea for a Universal History from a Cosmopolitan Point of View," in *Kant on History*, ed. Lewis White Beck (Indianapolis: Bobbs-Merrill Publishers, 1963), p. 15.

40. Ibid., p. 16.

41. Ibid., p. 15.

42. Ibid.

43. Ibid.

44. Plato, *The Collected Dialogues*, p. 710, #470e.

45. Kant, "Idea for a Universal History from a Cosmopolitan Point of View," p. 16.

46. Cornel West, *Prophetic Thought in Postmodern Times* (Monroe, Maine: Common Courage Press, 1993), p. 7.

47. Kant, "Review of Herder's Ideas for a Philosophy of the History of Mankind," p. 51.

48. Ironically enough, Léopold Sedar Senghor has made this very "difference" the positive embodiment of the being of the Negro African in his version of Négritude. For a

detailed appraisal of this point, see Tsenay Serequeberhan, *The Hermeneutics of African Philosophy* (New York: Routledge, 1994), pp. 42–53.

49. G. W. F. Hegel, *The Philosophy of History,* trans. J. Sibree (New York: Dover Publishers, Inc., 1956), p. 99.

50. Ibid., p. 98.

51. *Hegel's Philosophy of Right,* trans. T. M. Knox (New York: Oxford University Press, 1976), pp. 151–52, paragraphs 246–48. For a detailed discussion of Hegel's colonialist bent, see Serequeberhan, "The Idea of Colonialism in Hegel's *Philosophy of Right.*"

52. *Hegel's Philosophy of Right,* p. 219, paragraph 351.

53. Ibid., p. 219, paragraph 350.

54. Ibid., p. 217, paragraph 347.

55. Hegel, *The Philosophy of History,* p. 11.

56. *Hegel's Philosophy of Right,* p. 253, paragraph 129.

57. Robert Bernasconi, "African Philosophy's Challenge to Continental Philosophy," in *Postcolonial African Philosophy: A Critical Reader,* ed. E. C. Eze (Cambridge, Mass.: Blackwell Publishers, 1997), p. 190.

58. Marcien Towa, "Propositions sur l'identité culturelle," *Présence Africaine* 109 (1st Quarter, 1979), p. 84.

59. Robert Bernasconi, "Can Development Theory Break with Its Past? Endogenous Development in Africa and the Old Imperialism," *African Philosophy* 11, no. 1 (June 1998), p. 26.

60. Karl Marx and Frederick Engels, *The German Ideology* (New York: International Publishers, 1993), p. 151. For a detailed discussion of Marx's Eurocentrism, see Serequeberhan, "Karl Marx and African Emancipatory Thought."

61. Quoted in Edward W. Said, *Orientalism* (New York: Vintage Books, 1979), p. 97.

62. Karl Marx and Frederick Engels, *The Communist Manifesto* (New York: International Publishers, 1988), p. 14, emphasis added.

63. Karl Marx, "The Future Results of British Rule in India," in *On Colonialism* (New York: International Publishers, 1972), p. 87.

64. Ibid., p. 82.

65. Ibid., p. 31.

66. Karl Marx, *Capital,* vol. 1, trans. Ben Fowkes (New York: Vintage Books, 1977), pp. 172–73; and *Pre-Capitalist Economic Formations,* introduction by Eric J. Hobsbawm (New York: International Publishers, 1975), p. 84.

67. Frederick Engels, *The Part Played by Labor in the Transition from Ape to Man* (written in 1876) (New York: International Publishers, 1950), p. 18.

68. Marx, "The Future Results of British Rule in India," p. 82.

69. Ibid., p. 85.

70. Vattimo, *Al di là del Soggetto,* p. 18.

71. Towa, "Propositions sur l'identité culturelle," p. 84.

72. Cornelius Castoriadis, "Reflections on 'Rationality' and 'Development': Presentation and Response to Critics," in *Philosophy, Politics, Autonomy,* ed. David Ames Curtis (New York and Oxford: Oxford University Press, 1991), p. 200.

73. Jean-François Lyotard, *Peregrinations Law, Form, Event* (New York: Columbia University Press, 1988), p. 18.

74. Frantz Fanon employs precisely this image of crippling to describe the condition of

the colonized in *Black Skin, White Masks*, trans. Charles Lam Markmann (New York: Grove Press, 1967), p. 140.

75. Towa, "Propositions sur l'identité culturelle," p. 83.

76. A. J. Barker, *The Rape of Ethiopia 1936* (New York: Ballantine Books, Inc., 1971), pp. 98–99.

77. Serequeberhan, *The Hermeneutics of African Philosophy*, p. 64.

78. Chinua Achebe, *Things Fall Apart* (New York: Anchor Books, 1994), p. 191.

79. Temples, *Bantu Philosophy*, p. 84.

80. Vattimo, *Al di là del Soggetto*, pp. 12–13.

81. Antonio Gramsci, "Oppressed and Oppressors," in *History, Philosophy and Culture in the Young Gramsci*, ed. P. Cavalcanti and P. Piccone (St. Louis: Telos Press, 1975), p. 156.

82. Amilcar Cabral, *Return to the Source: Selected Speeches* (New York: Monthly Review Press, 1973), p. 79, emphasis added.

CONCLUSION

1. Hans-Georg Gadamer, *Truth and Method* (New York: Crossroad Publishers, 1982), p. 15.

2. Frantz Fanon, *Peau noire masques blancs* (Paris: Éditions du Seuil, 1952), p. 16.

3. Chinua Achebe, *Anthills of the Savannah* (New York: Anchor Books, 1989), p. 210.

4. Quoted in Drew A. Hyland, *The Origins of Philosophy* (New York: Capricorn Books, 1973), p. 92.

5. Edward W. Said, "Yeats and Decolonization," in *Nationalism, Colonialism and Literature*, ed. and introduction by Seamus Deane (Minneapolis: University of Minnesota Press, 1992), p. 71.

6. Gianni Vattimo, *La società trasparente* (Milan: Garzanti Editore, 1989), pp. 10–11, emphasis added.

7. Ibid., p. 13, emphasis added. The phrase *hanno preso la parola* in the way that Vattimo makes use of it has the sense of snatching, grabbing, or seizing something (in this case, the word) by force.

8. Frantz Fanon, *Pour la révolution africaine* (Paris: François Maspero, 1964), p. 211.

9. Amilcar Cabral, *Return to the Source: Selected Speeches* (New York and London: Monthly Review Press, 1973), p. 88, emphasis added; see also *Our People Are Our Mountains* (Nottingham, U.K.: Russell Press, 1971), pp. 21–22.

10. Aimé Césaire, *Lettre à Maurice Thorez* (Paris: Présence Africaine, 1956), passim.

11. Friedrich Nietzsche, *The Gay Science* (New York: Vintage Books, 1974), no. 108, p. 167.

12. Okonda w'oleko Okolo, *Pour une philosophie de la culture et du développement: Recherches d'herméneutique et de praxis africaines* (Kinshasa: Presses Universitaires du Zaire, 1986), p. 46.

Index

Abyssinia, 50, 56
Achebe, Chinua, 40, 44, 58, 69, 74
action, xiv
Africa: Arab, 1; autonomy of, 77n5; contemporary, 35, 36, 41; dependence on colonizers, 3, 53, 57; enslavement of, 56; identity and, 41–43 (*see also* identity, African); modernization and, 40–41; "natural" status of, 66; political independence of, xii, 4; postcolonial, 8, 39–41; spiritual beliefs, 38–39; sub-Saharan, 1; systems of thought, 37, 38, 53; underdevelopment of, 57, 58; Western domination of, 5, 39–41, 53–54, 56–57
African Americans: heritage of struggle, 33–34; maintenance of humanity of and by, 17, 20; racism-defined existence, 17, 18–19; self-formation, 14–16, 17, 19, 20–22
Africans: internalization of colonial dominion, 4–6, 44, 54; self-formation, 39, 40, 43, 74; situation of, 56–57; Westernized, 3–6, 12, 54, 73
Afwerki, Isayas, 41, 43
American Negro Academy, 14, 15
Angelou, Maya, 34
anticolonialism, xii, 10. *See also* colonialism
Appiah, Kwame Anthony, 35; on African identity, 41–43, 74; on African philosophy, 37–38; on Du Bois, 13, 17, 19, 20,

23; on multiple spiritual forces, 38–39, 87n30
Arendt, Hannah, xiv, 60
Asanti Twi, 38
attributes, human, 16

barbarians, 61, 66. *See also* Other
Barker, A. J., 69
being-in-the-world, 20
Bernasconi, Robert, 58
Bildung, 16, 73
Blum, Lawrence, 35

Cabral, Amilcar, 40, 41, 55, 58; on ideology, 76; on violence, 70–71
capitalism, 57, 67
Castoriadis, Cornelius, 47, 50, 51, 68
Césaire, Aimé, xi, 3, 76; on Négritude, 16, 23, 44
Char, Réne, xi, xiv
Christianity, 50
civil rights movement (U.S.), xii
colonialism: defeat of, 12; effects of, 1, 2; Hegel and, 66; Marx and, 67, 68; philosophical justification/sanction for, xiv, 60, 66–68; refusal of, 9–10; Westernization and, 74–75
commodification, 40
conscience, 7–8
consciousness, 26–29; forms of, 28; freedom/autonomy of, 25, 26; self-constitution of, 26

About the Author

Tsenay Serequeberhan is a teacher of philosophy whose work is focused on Continental and African philosophy. He has taught at Boston College, the University of Massachusetts (Boston), Hampshire College, Simmons College, and Brown University. Serequeberhan is the author of *The Hermeneutics of African Philosophy: Horizon and Discourse* (1994) and the editor of *African Philosophy: The Essential Readings* (1991). He is presently working on a study focused on a reading of the core figures of the Continental tradition.

DATE DUE
